POCAHONTAS

Her Life & Legend

William M. S. Rasmussen

Robert S. Tilton

PUBLISHED FOR AN EXHIBITION

AT THE

VIRGINIA HISTORICAL SOCIETY,

RICHMOND

---

24 OCTOBER 1994-30 APRIL 1995

SUPPORTED BY A GRANT

FROM SIGNET BANK

with additional support from

The Walt Disney Company

VIRGINIA HISTORICAL SOCIETY

RICHMOND ✳ 1994

Foreword

*F*or several generations of school children all over the United States, the story has become a staple in their history classes, and as such it is an American legend. Captain John Smith, captured by the Powhatan Indians and scheduled for execution, is rescued at the last moment by the pleas of a lovely young "Indian princess" named Pocahontas. Her kindly act saves Smith, but more importantly, by marrying another Englishman, John Rolfe, she played a key role in restoring good relations between her father's people and those in the Jamestown settlement. ✳ How accurate is the story? Is it more myth than reality? And why is it that Pocahontas has captured the imagination of Americans almost longer than anyone else in our history? Does her story help us better understand American Indians or is it more instructive of the dominant white society both during and long after her lifetime? These are but a few of the questions that are addressed in the exhibition entitled "Pocahontas: Her Life and Legend" and in this catalogue. While the exhibition may not dispel the myths of Pocahontas, we hope that it will help explain why they were created and why they have endured so long and so intensely. ✳ In this exhibition, the Virginia Historical Society has brought together a remarkable collection of images and objects, some of which have never been on public display before. We are indebted to a number of lending institutions and private owners for making these important items available to us. The exhibition and the catalogue would not have been possible without the strong financial support of Signet Bank; additional funding for the catalogue was provided by The Walt Disney Company. The people of Virginia are the chief beneficiaries of their generosity in backing this project. ✳ Finally, I want to thank the co-curators, Dr. William M. S. Rasmussen, Virginius C. Hall Curator of Art at the Historical Society, and Dr. Robert S. Tilton, professor of American literature at Queens College in New York and a noted scholar on the Pocahontas legend. Their solid scholarship and creativity have resulted in a thoroughly educational, yet entertaining exhibition. Other members of our staff have made important contributions to its success, namely project director Dr. James C. Kelly, registrar Giles Cromwell, and exhibits preparator Dale Kostelny. Thanks to the hard work of everyone involved in "Pocahontas: Her Life and Legend," all of us will gain a fuller understanding of a subject that in many ways has been an enigma for nearly four centuries.

Charles F. Bryan, Jr.

Charles F. Bryan, Jr.
DIRECTOR

Library of Congress Catalog Card Number: 94-61248
ISBN 0-945015-09-7

Production supervisor: Don J. Beville
Catalog design: Linda B. Berry

Printed in the United States of America

Lenders to the Exhibition

- ABBY ALDRICH ROCKEFELLER FOLK ART CENTER

- AMERICAN ILLUSTRATORS GALLERY

- ASSOCIATION FOR THE PRESERVATION OF VIRGINIA ANTIQUITIES

- CHRYSLER MUSEUM

- WILLIAM W. COLE

- COLLEGE OF WILLIAM AND MARY

- THE WALT DISNEY COMPANY

- HENRICO COUNTY

- MR. & MRS. WILLIAM MAURY HILL

- HISTORICAL SOCIETY OF PENNSYLVANIA

- MARY ELLEN HOWE

- JAMESTOWN SETTLEMENT MUSEUM COLLECTION

- KENDALL WHALING MUSEUM

- LIBRARY OF VIRGINIA

- HARRY & CONNIE LOCKWOOD'S MIDWESTERN GALLERIES

- PAGE MANN

- MASSACHUSETTS HISTORICAL SOCIETY

- ROBERT MEGANCK

- MUSEUM OF THE CONFEDERACY

- NATIONAL MUSEUM OF AMERICAN HISTORY

- NATIONAL PORTRAIT GALLERY, WASHINGTON, D.C.

- NEW-YORK HISTORICAL SOCIETY

- NEW YORK PUBLIC LIBRARY

- NEW YORK STATE EXECUTIVE MANSION, ALBANY

- THE GERALD PETERS GALLERY

- THE PETERSBURG MUSEUMS

- THE MORGAN RANK GALLERY

- WILLIAM E. RYDER

- SALISBURY STATE UNIVERSITY

- R THAD TAYLOR

- ROBERT S. AND RITA A. TILTON

- UNIVERSITY OF VIRGINIA

- VALENTINE MUSEUM

- VIRGINIA DEPARTMENT OF HISTORIC RESOURCES

- VIRGINIA MUSEUM OF FINE ARTS

- NICOLAS WINDISCH-GRAETZ

Introduction

"WHEN I THINK OF POCAHONTAS I AM READY TO LOVE INDIANS."

—Herman Melville, *The Confidence Man* (1857)[1]

She has been called America's Joan of Arc because of her saintlike virtue and her courage to risk death for a noble cause.[2] She has even been revered as the "mother" of the nation, the female counterpart to George Washington. Her rescue of Captain John Smith is one of the most famous and appealing episodes in all of our history. Few figures from the American past are better known than the young Powhatan woman who has come down to us as "Pocahontas."

She was born into a culture that had some knowledge of Europeans, and after their settling on the outskirts of the territory controlled by her father, she was apparently drawn to these peculiar strangers. A number of the chroniclers of the Jamestown founding mention her by name and note her interactions with the English settlers. This Powhatan girl, who was reported to have saved John Smith from execution and to have enjoyed cartwheeling naked with the young boys of the Jamestown settlement, would as a young woman be kidnapped as a political pawn, converted to Christianity, married to a settler, and taken to England as an example of the potential of the New World for cultural indoctrination. It was among members of her adopted nation that she took sick and died, at age twenty-two, as she attempted to return to her homeland.

The fame of Pocahontas began in her own lifetime. Contemporary Londoners welcomed with excitement a figure who was living proof that American natives could be Christianized and civilized. By the beginning of the eighteenth century, the reputation of Pocahontas was well established. Readers in England and on the Continent had come across her exploits in the popular travel literature of the period, and vignettes of her life had

been included on maps of the New World.[3] Robert Beverley reverently told of her in his history of Virginia; Joseph Addison honored her in an essay in the Spectator; and a Boston schoolgirl painted her portrait.[4] As Europeans of the eighteenth century looked back to the natural nobility of "primitive" cultures, the legend of the virtuous Pocahontas served as a useful model.

The nineteenth century saw the greatest dissemination of the Pocahontas legend. This was the period in which the brief history of America came to be recognized as containing the types of elements that could be used in the construction of romantic visual and literary narratives. During the first decade of the century her story had been wrestled from the exclusive purview of historians by novelists and dramatists, who had noted the potential in the great events of her life for stirring fictional portrayals. Portraitists rendered her image, and history painters recreated and glamorized her accomplishments. Politicians debating the "Indian problem," abolitionists, and sectionalists all manipulated her story for their own devices, and her likeness was to be seen on numerous advertisements for tobacco and medicine. Vessels of various sorts were named after both Pocahontas and Powhatan, as trains would be in the twentieth century. Towns, cities, and counties also adopted the names of the great Indian figures of Jamestown. The world record as the fastest horse in harness was held by the great pacing mare Pocahontas from 1855 to 1867. And while historians hotly debated the credibility of Smith's record of her life, one company of Confederate soldiers carried her image on a ceremonial banner.

Over the centuries since its creation, the Pocahontas narrative has so often been retold and embellished and so frequently adapted to contemporary issues that the actual, flesh-and-blood woman has long been hidden by the ever-burgeoning mythology. Today, as we prepare for the four hundredth anniversary of her birth in 1995, many questions about the historical figure of Pocahontas remain. This young woman, who was known among her own people as "Matoaka" and whose nickname was "Pocahontas" ("little wanton" or "little plaything"),[5] was an eyewitness to the convergence of two disparate cultures. Although she apparently possessed a number of extraordinary qualities, including a spirited and engaging personality,[6] it must be remembered that what we know about her has been lifted from the narratives of English males, all of whom brought their particular fantasies and prejudices to bear on their representations of the New World and its people. The daughter of Powhatan, whom Europeans dubbed a "king" and an "emperor," which made his daughter a "princess," left no words of her own. Her entire story is culled from these chronicles, and so an adequate reconstruction of her day-to-day life is not possible. What we can do, however, in our attempt to shed some light on this subject is to examine briefly the Powhatan culture that produced her. We will then go on to discuss the few events from her narrative that have formed the basis for her mythic status. Along the way we will often invoke the primary documents and note how the representations tend to grow farther removed from what "facts" were provided by her contemporaries.[7]

POCAHONTAS:
The Historical Record

Women in Powhatan Society

The land that today is Virginia and North Carolina was inhabited by Algonquian-speaking peoples when Europeans first arrived. Images of the appearance and life-style of these Native Americans were taken in 1585-86 by John White, an English artist and governor of the Roanoke Island settlement in what is now the Outer Banks of North Carolina. White, a talented painter who probably trained as a miniaturist, no doubt was following instructions to record what was strange to English eyes in the people, flora and fauna, and landscape of America. He worked side by side with Thomas Harriot, a scientist who wrote a text that complements the illustrations. Both spent the winter of 1585-86 in Tidewater Virginia, along what was later named the Elizabeth River, where they found a culture that was probably very similar to that later described by John Smith. Harriot's *Briefe and True Report of the New Found Land of Virginia* was published, with White's illustrations as engravings, in 1590 as the first part of *America*, a series about the New World produced by Theodor de Bry (1528-1598), a Flemish emigrant in Germany.

As depicted by the brush of John White, a Powhatan girl wore no clothing before puberty ✳ (fig.1). At about age twelve she would begin to dress as an adult. Her daily garment then was a deerskin apron, which could be decorated (here, with rows of beads at the top and bottom). Some of these aprons were "carved and couloured" with "pretty [pattern] work" or with images of animals ("beasts, fowle, tortayses, or other such imagry"). The lower edge was often "shagged and fringed." In the winter, a mantle, also of deerskin, was draped over one shoulder. Oil was sometimes applied to the skin as a second method of combating cold temperatures.[8]

Just as the deerskin aprons could be painted to add "colour," so could the bodies of Powhatan women. They customarily tattooed themselves, and on a daily

8

Figure 1 ✹ *John White,* INDIAN WOMAN AND YOUNG GIRL, *1585-86, watercolor, 10 ³/₈ x 5 ⁷/₈ in. Courtesy of the British Museum.*

basis they added body paint that was derived from various roots. As shown by White, nearly all portions of skin not covered by the apron could be "cuningly imbrodered" by applying "sondry coulers [colors]" to punctures pierced by a heated "instrument," usually a sharply pointed bone. The tattoos were often geometric. Other times, they copied designs from nature, such as "flowers and fruits . . . , as also snakes, serpents, eftes [lizards]," "Fowls, Fish or Beasts."⁹

To compensate for the simplicity and the necessarily monotonous regularity of their dress, Powhatan Indians indulged their love of jewelry, which they valued highly. Women wore multiple necklaces, as well as bracelets and earrings. These were strung with pearls, shell beads, copper, animal teeth, or beads of bone. Though the pearls were often low grade, they were intricately worked. Both round beads and long pipe beads were laboriously crafted out of shells, as were coin-shaped pendants (sometimes called discs or frontals), which were also worn as necklaces.

According to White's depictions, the hair of a Powhatan woman was cut close, except at the back. Alternative styles were the extremes of a "bowl" haircut or long hair loose to the waist. On some occasions there might be "some variety of feathers, and flowers

stuck in their haires."¹⁰ The women not only tended their own hair, but they were also often given the responsibility of cutting the hair of their husbands.

White's watercolors also portray a life-style for Indian women that it is safe to assume was similar to that in which Pocahontas was raised. His view of the village of Secoton, on what is now the mainland of North Carolina ✹ (fig. 2), documents an apparently physically demanding existence. To match the conspicuous contributions of their husbands, who served as warriors, hunters, and fishermen, women of the Powhatan nation assumed the great majority of the remaining workload.

The women took on the arduous duty of house building for their families. A Powhatan house was made

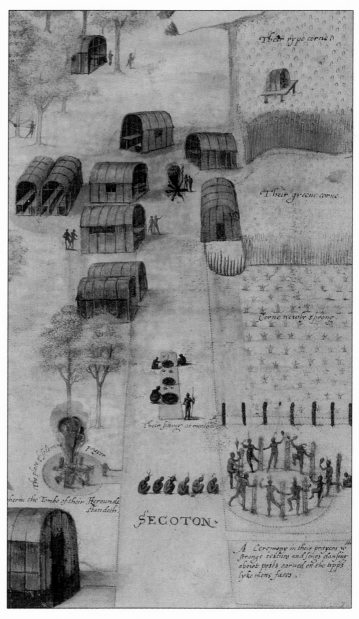

Figure 2 ✹ *John White,* INDIAN VILLAGE OF SECOTON, *1585-86, watercolor, 12 ³/₄ x 7 ³/₄ in. Courtesy of the British Museum.*

of cut saplings bent at the top to form barrel vaults. For the covering and flooring of the house, bark was peeled and mats woven out of straws and grasses. Bending the wood minimized cutting, which was particularly demanding given the unsophisticated cutting tools known to their culture. The implements that existed were made by the women from stones, shells, and bones and teeth of animals. In addition to maintaining a semipermanent residence, it also fell to the woman to pack up their belongings and move the household seasonally to temporary settings, where new shelters had to be erected. In such moves they followed the hunters in search of the plentiful deer population.

Powhatan women also did the farming for their tribes. White's watercolor of Secoton show May, June, and July crops of corn, which were planted and harvested by the women, as were tobacco and food crops, such as pumpkins and sunflowers. Those who could grow large quantities of corn were respected, for the crop was valued as wealth. During the periods between harvests, or when crops were ripening, women gathered wild plant foods, such as berries and nuts.

The women's responsibility for food preparation is illustrated by White. They prepared and served all foods and made the implements used for food production and preparation. Women built both cooking pots (out of coiled clay) and the fires for cooking ✳ (fig. 3). They shaped wood, gourds, and shells into dishes, spoons, and ladles and worked turtle shells into cups. By his glance, the male figure in "Their sitting at meate" seems to betray his debt to his mate ✳ (fig. 4). To be sure, he had hunted the animal whose meat they eat and whose skin they wear, but she had done the rest. She prepared and cooked the meal, made their deerskin clothing, and even the mat on which they sit.

Pocahontas from the Contemporary Sources

Only scattered references to the appearance and character of Pocahontas have survived. Although little is known about the day-to-day life of Pocahontas, the major events were noted, if not actually witnessed, by various Englishmen. William Strachey, in his rendition of the early days of the Virginia colony, provided the shocking depiction of the naked young girl cavorting with the boys of the settlement, as well as the report that she had been married to an Indian named Kocoum.[11] His text, however, was only rediscovered in 1849 and so was not available to those who romanticized her story in the early nineteenth century. Ralph Hamor provided much of what we know about her kidnapping and gave details about her marriage. This report was augmented by the accounts of Sir Thomas Dale, Alexander Whitaker, and her husband John Rolfe, all of whom also provide information about her conversion. The prolific letter writer John Chamberlain supplied some information about her stay in England, which was also mentioned by Samuel Purchas, among others. Simon van de Passe depicted "Matoaka als Rebecka" in a 1616 engraving and so provided the only likeness contrived during her lifetime, though this portrayal may be unrepresentative because it gives us the daughter of "Powhatan Emperour of Attanoughkomouck" as the Virginia Company, her sponsor, and the artist wanted her to be seen ✳ (fig. 5).

The chief architect of the Pocahontas legend, however, is Captain John Smith, who in his *Generall Historie*, written in 1624 after the deaths of all of the other principals, first publicized the story of his sur-

Figure 3 ✳ *John White,* COOKING IN A POT, *1585-86, watercolor, 5 ⅞ x 7 ⅝ in. Courtesy of the British Museum.*

Figure 4 ✳ *John White,* INDIAN MAN AND WOMAN EATING, *1585-86, watercolor, 8 ¼ x 8 ½ in. Courtesy of the British Museum.*

prising rescue by a heroic Indian girl. He also retrospectively filled in some of the gaps in her story and provided some new information about her adventures in England.

Although the trustworthiness of all of these accounts can be called into question, they form the foundations around which are built later, more elaborate renditions. That verifiable "facts" are few and far between proved in a way to be a boon to the literary and visual artists who wished to tell the story of the "rescue," or her baptism, or her marriage, because they were therefore free to depict these events in whatever form they wished. By the end of the nineteenth century, although their historical veracity was still at times debated, their truth as sources had grown beyond the power of those who would attempt to demythologize the heroine of Jamestown.

Figure 5 ✳ *Simon van de Passe,* POCAHONTAS, *1616, engraving, 6 ¾ x 4 ¾ in., published in John Smith's* Generall Historie, *1624. Virginia Historical Society, photograph by Katherine Wetzel.*

Episodes from the Life of
POCAHONTAS

Captain John Smith

Much of what we know about Pocahontas comes from the pen of John Smith ✳ (fig. 6), a larger-than-life figure who became a writer in order to record his observations and experiences in the New World. Smith was born in Willoughby, Lincolnshire, England, in 1580. Although he has come to be best known through his accounts of his experiences in America, before ever setting foot in Virginia, Smith, by his own admission, had already endured adventures that would have filled more than one ordinary lifetime. In his autobiographical *True Travels* he reported that he had fought in eastern Europe in the Hungarian wars against the Turks. In single combats before audiences of both armies he had defeated and beheaded three Turkish champions. Later, after he had been wounded in battle and left to die, Smith was captured and sold into slavery. He escaped from bondage in Istanbul through the good offices of the Lady Tragabigzanda, the wife of a Turkish pasha, who had fallen in love with him. In Russia he was again enslaved, only to escape by killing his master and setting off across Europe. Already a seasoned warrior on his arrival in Virginia, the twenty-seven-year-old Smith quickly observed that the courage of an Indian was fueled by a show of fear on the part of his adversary: "their courages to proceede [comes] from others feare." Accordingly, Smith showed only brashness and bravery to the Powhatans and so won their highest respect. He became an almost legendary figure to them, one "admired . . . as a demi-God" and remembered for years after he had left Virginia.[12]

Smith's brashness, which resulted perhaps as much from his personality as from his experiences, earned him legions of enemies among both the Jamestown colonists

Figure 6 ✳ Simon van de Passe, CAPTAIN JOHN SMITH, *1616, engraving, 4 ³/₄ x 3 ³/₈ in., published as part of the map of New England in John Smith's* Generall Historie, *1624. Virginia Historical Society, photograph by Katherine Wetzel.*

and the London circle of the Virginia Company. While some of the former resented his leadership and abilities, many of the latter who were of high social standing looked down on his yeoman background. His talents, however, became crucial during the earliest days of the settlement, and he quickly became the actual, if not the nominal, leader of the expedition.

Modern scholars are as divided about Smith as were his contemporaries. He has long been discredited as a historian, often because there were no corroborative witnesses to the events he reported. Today, his accounts are often believed, if only because there are few

obvious inaccuracies in the information that he provided. Although there is no doubt that he was a shameless self-promoter, who probably thought himself the most able man in any room, he was also apparently a soldier of exceptional talent, a natural leader, an amateur ethnologist of some ability who was sufficiently sensitive to Indian behavior to understand Virginia's native population, and an able diplomat who maintained relations with the Powhatans and thereby saved the fledgling colony from destruction.

Many professional ethnologists, who reconstruct cultures on the basis of factual evidence, see Smith differently. They are reluctant to trust what often appears to be dubious information that cannot be corroborated through archaeological or historical sources, especially when it was provided by an egotist who was often abrasive and insensitive to the Indian population. Only by today's standards, however, was John Smith insensitive to the Powhatan culture. Indeed, he was surprisingly unprejudiced when compared to much of the society from which he sprang. He was sufficiently well traveled to expect racial and cultural diversity and sufficiently shrewd to comprehend the importance of understanding cultural differences. He was one of the few colonists who learned to speak the Algonquian language, and he reported, with minimal bias, a wide range of information about Powhatan life. Although noting his own abilities to circumvent their strategies, he gave Indian leaders, and especially Powhatan himself, credit for intelligence and sagacity. Indeed, he treated Indians little differently than he treated whites, which perhaps explains his lack of popularity among many of the settlers, even though he proved to be one of their most humane and fair leaders.

THE RESCUE OF CAPTAIN JOHN SMITH

DATE: December 1607

PLACE: Powhatan's village of Werowocomoco on the York River

RECORDED: John Smith's letter to Anne of Denmark; Smith's *Generall Historie* (1624)[13]

John Smith's *Generall Historie*, in which he first described the rescue scene as it has been mythologized, also contains a double page of crude engravings of half a dozen of the more dramatic adventures of the author. At the lower right is a depiction of the rescue of Smith by Pocahontas ✳ (fig. 7). Because this scene was so strange and depicted a previously unknown event, the engraver felt compelled to identify what he had taken from Smith's account.

To summarize briefly what the captain recorded, he and his exploring party were intercepted along the Chickahominy River west of Jamestown by Powhatan

Figure 7 ✳ *Robert Vaughan,* KING POWHATAN COMANDS C. SMITH TO BE SLAYNE, HIS DAUGHTER POKAHONTAS BEGGS HIS LIFE . . . , *1624, engraving, 4 ³/₈ x 3 ⁷/₈ in., published in John Smith's* Generall Historie, 1624. *Virginia Historical Society, photograph by Katherine Wetzel.*

Indians who were apparently engaged in an intertribal winter hunt. Smith "was beset with 200 Salvages, two of them hee slew." Others he maimed with pistol fire while holding one of his Indian guides as a human shield, "till at last they tooke him prisoner." For the next several weeks "many strange triumphes and conjurations they made of him." He recorded more than once that "at each place I expected . . . they would execute me."[14]

Smith's captor, and the leader of the hunting party, was Opechancanough, Powhatan's half brother. He escorted the captive Smith through a number of villages where he was displayed and examined. At one, priests conducted a three-day ritual to determine "if he [Smith] intended them well or no."[15] If they reached a conclusion about the intentions of Smith and the English, the captain did not record it.

Finally, Smith was taken to Werowocomoco and presented to Powhatan. The king impressed Smith with his "grave and Majesticall countenance"—an aspect of Powhatan that was far beyond the talents of the engraver of the *Generall Historie*. Along each side of the house were "two rowes of men, and behind them as many women." After a "long consultation,"

> *two great stones were brought before Powhatan: then as many as could layd hands on him [Smith], dragged him to them, and thereon laid his head, and being ready with their clubs, to beate out his braines, Pocahontas the Kings dearest daughter, when no intreaty could prevaile, got his head in her armes, and laid her owne*

upon his to save him from death: whereat the Emperour was contented he should live to make him hatchets, and her bells, beads, and copper.[16]

Other than its place as the first depiction of the rescue scene, the 1624 image does not hold great visual interest. Indeed, this work is something of a composite. Elements such as the hall and the figure of Powhatan were based on earlier representations. Over the following 380 years, however, numerous artists would provide their interpretations of this dramatic event.

After Theodor de Bry's death in 1598, his *America* series of eventually fourteen volumes was continued by his family. The history of the Jamestown founding was included, but its representation did not have the accuracy of the Roanoke Island illustrations taken from John White's on-site drawings. One of the episodes chosen by the de Brys was Smith's capture and rescue ✳ (fig. 8). The engraver illustrates three successive incidents drawn from Smith's report of this

Figure 8 ✳ *Unknown artist,* THE CAPTURE, EVALUATION, AND RESCUE OF JOHN SMITH, *1634, engraving, 6 x 7 in., published in the de Bry family,* America, *13. Courtesy of the Tracy W. McGregor Library of American History, Special Collections, University of Virginia Library.*

episode and he is faithful to Smith's account in nearly every detail.

In the distant background is the earliest event: Smith, after his capture, is led to Opechancanough's hunting village. The artist illustrates the processional: "drawing themselves all in fyle, . . . Smith was led . . . by . . . great Salvages, holding him fast by each arme."[17] So engrossing was the next incident to Smith's contemporaries that the de Brys gave it the entire right half of

13

the composition. This is the divining ritual performed by exotic Indian priests to evaluate the threat posed by the Englishman. They laid out meal, corn, and sticks to represent their country, the sea, and the land from whence came the English intruders. The artist follows Smith's descriptions of these figures and their attire, as well as the paraphernalia of the scene, which includes bows and arrows, clubs, birds, and animal skins.

The left middleground is given to the rescue by Pocahontas, which was performed days later at Powhatan's village, Werowocomoco. The artist is faithful to Smith's account of the "two great stones" brought for his execution, the warriors, "ready with their clubs, to beate out his braines," and Pocahontas herself, who lays "her owne [head] upon his to save him from death." Also shown here are the "grim Courtiers [who] stood wondering at him, as he had beene a monster."[18]

Over the next 200 years there would be other representations of the "rescue," but these were often based on their seventeenth-century predecessors and do little to expand on the traditional renderings. It was not until the early nineteenth century, when the rescue of John Smith could be placed within the chain of events that led to the founding of the American republic, that visual artists, following on the heels of the British expatriate writer John Davis, who had featured elaborated versions of this scene in his attempts to expand the Pocahontas narrative into a full-fledged romance, felt free to make their own structural and thematic additions to this scene.[19] Chief among these additions was that it was romantic love for the handsome captain in the bosom of the twelve- or thirteen-year-old princess that was the motivating force behind her display of heroism.[20] In 1804 Virginia historian John Burk saw this scene as a vehicle fit for the talents of a true master:

> *The spectacle of Pocahontas in an attitude of entreaty, with her hair loose, and her eyes streaming with tears, . . . is a situation equal to the genius of Raphael: And when the royal savage directs his ferocious glance for a moment, from his victim, to reprove his weeping daughter . . . , the painter will discover a new occasion for exercising his talents.*[21]

By the early 1800s, the rescue of John Smith had become well known through its appearances in the fiction of Davis, in dramas such as *The Indian Princess* by James Nelson Barker, in entries about Smith or Pocahontas in biographical dictionaries, and in a number of the popular histories of the period.[22] The reception of this scene is evidenced by its being chosen as fitting for inclusion in the United States Capitol. In 1825 Antonio Capellano, one of several foreign sculptors drawn to the new republic, carved in relief a rendi-

tion of the "rescue" that he made simple and bold, so that it would fit the square space given the artist and be easily identifiable high above the western door of the rotunda ✳ (fig. 9). Its derivation from the "rude engraving" in Smith's *Generall Historie* is confirmed by the 1830 guidebook to the Capitol.[23] The relief is a powerful piece of sculpture by a competent artist, who chose to emphasize the response of the "grim courtiers" to the raised hand of Powhatan, rather than his response to his daughter's action.

Figure 9 ✳ *Antonio Capellano,* PRESERVATION OF CAPTAIN SMITH BY POCAHONTAS. *1825, sandstone, U.S. Capitol Rotunda. Courtesy of the Architect of the Capitol.*

The rescue of John Smith was the subject of a number of popular prints during the mid-nineteenth century.[24] One of the more interesting of these is Thomas Sinclair's lithograph produced for James Wimer's *Events in Indian History* ✳ (fig. 10). Sinclair saw the captain as a handsome young officer. His Smith is dressed and groomed not in Jacobean fashion but in that of the early nineteenth century. The figure of Pocahontas is petite, beautiful, and seemingly Caucasian. Sinclair may have believed that his rendering of this attractive pair, whose romance was intertwined with momentous historical events, would find admirers among both the readers of Sir Walter Scott and the large, often female, readership of sentimental fiction in America. He clearly feels that the historical inaccuracy of his casting would have been insignificant to the majority of Wimer's readers.

In 1845, believing that no artist of "genius, taste and imagination" had painted this scene, William Gilmore Simms, one of the most important southern literary figures of the antebellum period, published an essay entitled "Pocahontas: A Subject For The Historical Painter." In this piece he reproached John Gadsby Chapman, who had chosen to paint the *Baptism of Pocahontas* to fill one of the vacant panels in the Capitol rotunda, for "avoid[ing] the nobler event" in the life of Pocahontas. Simms, who invited Chapman to attempt a "rescue,"[25] was clearly unaware that the artist had already painted two versions of this scene, in 1835 and 1836 ❋ (fig. 11). (Both paintings had passed directly to private collectors, and an engraving after the later version was never widely circulated.)[26]

Many of Simms's suggestions had been anticipated by Chapman. Simms said that the history painter must use wise judgment to choose the precise moment when the drama is at its height, "to catch the vivid emotion and the hungry passion, ere they subside into the repose which follows from natural exhaustion." That instant in the "rescue" scene is when the "dilating but tearless eyes" of Pocahontas turn to "the fierce old monarch."[27] Chapman was the first artist of note to depict their moment of interaction.

Simms described Pocahontas as a "vision of light and beauty" at these "dark proceedings."[28] This was precisely the image that Chapman had conceived al-

Figure 10 ❋ *Thomas Sinclair,* CAPTAIN SMITH RESCUED BY POCAHONTAS, *1841, lithograph, 11 x 12 in., published in James Wimer's* Events of Indian History, *1841. Courtesy of the Library of Virginia.*

most ten years before Simms's essay. As in a scene by Caravaggio of the martyrdom of a saint, Chapman silhouettes Pocahontas against a cloud of white smoke and bathes her in light. The smoke and light seem to sanctify her. This treatment is appropriate for the savior both of Smith's life and of the Indians, who are saved from the savage act of executing their prisoner. Diagonal lines intensify the drama while they stabilize

Figure 11 ❋ *John Gadsby Chapman,* POCAHONTAS SAVING THE LIFE OF CAPTAIN JOHN SMITH. *1836, oil on canvas, 21 x 25 ¼ in. Courtesy of the New-York Historical Society.*

the scene. A number of elements, including the exposed-beam interior, the fire, and Powhatan's feathered headdress, derive from the 1624 engraving ✳ (fig. 7).

In 1861 Alonzo Chappel depicted the same scene as one of the dozens he conceived as illustrations for the sumptuous American history books of the period ✳ (fig. 12).[29] No doubt the artist had little time or much reason to research a scene already developed by Chapman. Chappel borrowed essential elements from Chapman's composition, including the exposed-beam

Figure 12 ✳ *Alonzo Chappel,* POCAHONTAS SAVING THE LIFE OF CAPT. JOHN SMITH. *1861, engraving, 7 ³/₈ x 5³/₈ in., published in J.A. Spencer,* History of the United States, *1866. Courtesy of Salisbury State University, Salisbury, Maryland, photograph by Katherine Wetzel.*

house and the centrally placed heroine backlit by white smoke from a campfire, but in this case the smoke takes on the characteristics of a halo. Also different, and more true to fact, Chappel makes Pocahontas a child and Smith a man some years her senior. Her impassioned stand against violence captures the attention of her father and thereby overpowers the influence of the sensual young women at his side. The structure in which Chappel's "rescue" takes place is far too large to have been architecturally correct, and the inappropriate paraphernalia, some of which would have been reminiscent of Plains Indian cultures, detract from the historical veracity of this dramatic and effective scene.

Chappel was not the only artist who included what were in the process of becoming generic "Indian" trappings in representations of the "rescue." Edward Corbould, a London painter who was prominent for his exhibition record and who served as art instructor to the children of Queen Victoria, strayed even farther from Smith's account. Though his Pocahontas painting is apparently lost, the image is preserved in paintings and engravings done after it, one of which is a large color lithograph by Christian Inger, published in 1870 by H. Schile of New York ✳ (fig. 13). Here, a great story is given the richest of treatments. Pocahontas saves Smith from beheading at the hand of Opechancanough, who wields a magnificent metal sword, a weapon as foreign to his civilization as are the rich costumes and the horses also offered.

To judge from an earlier print after Corbould by T. Wright, Inger chose to expand on an already outlandish scene. He exaggerates costumes that are already overly exotic, adds tepees, and beside Powhatan inserts a figure at the far left whom he identifies as Namontack, the name of a historical Indian who later served as an emissary for Powhatan in England. Probably by chance alone some of the figures are appropriately underclothed, and parts of the landscape bear a resemblance to the green forests of Virginia. The large number of generic Indian devices in this depiction, from the tepees, horses, and headdresses to his overly nubile princess, point to the standardization of such popular images and to the process that was beginning to make Plains Indians the models for all native cultures. Such representations also deftly connect the Anglo-American successes in Virginia to contemporary

Figure 13 ✳ *Christian Inger (after Edward Corbould),* SMITH RESCUED BY POCAHONTAS. *1870, lithograph, 18 x 24 ³/₄ in., published by H. Schile, Virginia Historical Society, photograph by Katherine Wetzel.*

American concerns about the fate of the Plains cultures and of the white settlers who live among them.

Victor Nehlig was a French history, portrait, and genre painter who had learned his trade on the Continent before settling in New York City. There he was elected an academician of the National Academy of Design in 1870, the year he showed his skills in a massive, seven-foot-tall vertical canvas in which he depicts Pocahontas saving John Smith.[30] Four years later he released a large lithograph that is a horizontal variation of the same scene ✳ (fig. 14). Although Nehlig provides the essential elements of the story, he feels free to augment the details. He presents Indians of the western plains, dressed in costumes as far removed from the Powhatan culture of eastern Virginia as is the rocky landscape on which they stand. Neither Smith nor Pocahontas bears any resemblance either to their engraved portraits or to their representations in the majority of the previous renderings of this scene. Indeed, Nehlig breaks the long tradition of having a rather well-developed Pocahontas kneeling over Smith, choosing instead to portray what might be an adolescent in full flight toward the intended victim.

The setting of an exposed beam house and the device of a backdrop of white smoke to accentuate and sanctify his heroine derive from the Chapman-Chappel tradition, but Nehlig goes further: he employs the artistic devices used by baroque painters of the Counter Reformation to maximize the emotional effect of scenes of martyrdom—a gigantic scale, bold compositional diagonals, and a dramatic interplay of light, shade, and space. If Nehlig's executioner seems savage, his depiction is not a comment on any contemporary Indian problems but rather a visualization of ferocity and power designed to instill awe in the viewer. If Powhatan has the regal presence of an Aztec king, if Pocahontas is portrayed at the moment of her leap into action, rather than as a still figure kneeling over Smith, and if the tribal group exudes rough splendor, those elements were conceived for their sensational effect. Nehlig, perhaps more than any artist who preceded him, succeeds in stretching the drama of the "rescue" scene to the limit.

Figure 14 ✳ *Victor Nehlig,* POCAHONTAS SAVING JOHN SMITH, *1874, lithograph, 22½ x 33 ½ in., published by F. Tuch Farber & Co., Virginia Historical Society, photograph by Katherine Wetzel.*

Did Pocahontas Rescue John Smith?

Nehlig's image is so fanciful that it raises the question whether the rescue of John Smith really happened. For the past century, many have wondered if it did.

Through much of the late 1800s, sectionalists feuded about the history and culture of the South—and about the Pocahontas story. New England historians Charles Deane and his disciple Henry Adams were intent on discrediting the South's efforts to formulate an impressive history of its own. In *The Education of Henry Adams* the author recalls John Gorham Palfrey's suggestion that an attack "on Captain John Smith's relations with Pocahontas would attract as much attention, and probably break as much glass, as any other stone that could be thrown by a beginner." He asserted to Palfrey in 1862 that "the Virginia aristocracy" would be "utterly gravelled" by such a disparagement. These Northern

17

historians ultimately succeeded in casting serious doubt about whether a rescue ever took place. In an 1867 article about Smith, Adams portrayed the Captain as an irresponsible liar.[31] Many historians think differently today, however. They find Smith to be validated at virtually every point on which he can be checked.

Ethnologists, on the other hand, are inclined to dismiss the rescue as highly problematical for a number of reasons: Smith did not mention the rescue in his earliest accounts that record his capture by Powhatan (*A True Relation* [1608] and *Proceedings . . . of the Colony* [1612]); Powhatan Indians did not welcome and eat with a captive whose death was imminent; Powhatan priests, who were highly influential in their society, had already examined Smith and—presumably, because they did not kill him—declared him acceptable; and if Smith was to have been executed, clubbing was not the means the Powhatans would have used. To the Indians' thinking, a quick death by clubbing or burning was a humiliation awarded petty criminals within the chiefdom; a worthy opponent, like Smith, would have rated the honorable experience of a slow and painful execution, which probably would have included flaying and dismemberment, with limbs thrown into a fire, followed by disembowelment.[32]

Sharing the ethnologists' suspicion that Smith's life was never in danger at Werowocomoco, some historians have suggested that the rescue was a ritual that the Englishman simply did not understand. Following that theory, Pocahontas served as a sponsor for Smith as he was adopted into Powhatan's tribe. Smith's death was ceremonial, a prelude to his rebirth into Indian society. Because this was only a ritual, no "rescue" actually took place.[33] The strongest challenge to the adoption theory comes from ethnologists, who point to the absence of evidence that the Powhatan Indians practiced such a ritual.

A final possibility is that the incident at Werowocomoco was a test of Smith's manliness and that the outcome of the incident was unresolved when Pocahontas intervened. Throughout their lives the courage of Powhatan men was under scrutiny. It was repeatedly tested, a reason they often similarly tested opponents through physical torture or the threat of it. To the thinking of the Powhatan Indian, an outsider deserved a test of manliness; if he failed it, he was an inferior.

Against the anthropological perspective, which would lead one to doubt the occurrence of a rescue, a series of arguments can be made that suggest that it did indeed take place:

An unusual relationship clearly existed between Smith and Pocahontas immediately after his captivity. Pocahontas became the emissary who accompanied Powhatan's provisions of food, and who carried to Jamestown a request for the release of Indian prison-

ers. So sudden and special a bond cannot be explained adequately unless it was formed while Smith was a prisoner.

Smith's account of the rescue was apparently accepted by his contemporaries, such as Samuel Purchas, who published accounts about Virginia and who interviewed in London principal figures involved in the Virginia settlement (including Pocahontas and John Rolfe), as well as other individuals who had played a part in Virginia's history, such as Samuel Argall and Ralph Hamor. Even Smith's enemies, people his brash behavior had offended, such as George Percy, who took issue in print in 1625 with some of the material in the *Generall Historie*, apparently did not take the time to publicly doubt the "rescue" story. In 1623, when he testified to a commission conducting an in-depth investigation of the Virginia Company, Smith credited the "King's daughter as the means to return me safe to James towne." He would hardly have lied to an investigative committee that had access to multiple witnesses with firsthand experience in Virginia.[34]

Did Pocahontas rescue Smith? The question may never be answered conclusively. The incidents of Powhatan Indian behavior that from an anthropological perspective are unusual, and thus suspicious, are disturbing. The historical evidence, however, is persuasive. Until proven otherwise, Pocahontas should probably be awarded credit for saving Smith, if only from a test of his composure under duress.

POCAHONTAS WARNS CAPTAIN JOHN SMITH

DATE: January 1609 (1608/9)

PLACE: Powhatan's village of Werowocomoco on the York River

RECORDED: John Smith's letter to Anne of Denmark; Smith's *Generall Historie* (1624); one sentence in Smith's *Proceedings . . . of the Colony* (1612)[35]

John Gadsby Chapman illustrated a series of episodes of the Pocahontas-Jamestown saga. In 1835 he painted a small *Rescue of John Smith* that was engraved and was a "companion" to *The Capture of Smith* that he also rendered. The next year he paired another two episodes that are sequential, *The Coronation of Powhatan* and *The Warning of Pocahontas*.[36] The former took place in October of 1608. Christopher Newport attempted to crown Powhatan as a vassal of King James I, but the ruler saw through the subterfuge and refused to assume the subordinate posture of kneeling. This incident could symbolize the deteriorating relations that made it necessary three months later for Pocahontas to warn Smith that her father again intended to kill him.

Chapman devised the composition of *The Warning of Pocahontas* ✳ (fig. 15) to complement *The Coronation of Powhatan*, which has the same dimensions and was sold to the same patron. Pocahontas lifts her arm

Pocahontas in the Capitol rotunda. That painting may have reawakened an interest in scenes from her life other than the "rescue." The large murals that were painted between 1836 and 1855 to fill the four vacant panels in the rotunda had been the nation's premier commissions for history paintings. White was certainly influenced by

Figure 15 ✳ *John Gadsby Chapman,* THE WARNING OF POCAHONTAS, *1836, oil on canvas 22 ½ x 29 in. Private collection, photograph courtesy of Gerald Peters Gallery, Santa Fe, New Mexico.*

in gesture, just as Newport raises high a crown for Powhatan. Chapman clearly had read Smith's account, for he shows the captain "quarter[ed] . . . in [one of] the King's [Powhatan's] houses," which is modeled after an illustration in the *Generall Historie*, and in the distance are the English barges mired in the frozen water that kept the party from fleeing Powhatan's village. Four of the eighteen men Smith brought ashore are depicted. For enhanced drama, they sleep through the incident like guards at the tomb in Renaissance paintings of Christ's resurrection. In fact, the time was not late night but early evening, before dinner.[37]

The "warning" scene holds interest for its drama while providing a challenge to the artist because the action is spoken and the setting is at night. Edwin White was drawn to this subject perhaps in part because of this very difficulty ✳ (fig. 16). He was a portrait and history painter who studied in Düsseldorf, where the vogue was to use chiaroscuro—contrasting extremes of light and dark emphasized primarily for dramatic effect—in the tradition of Rembrandt's paintings of biblical scenes.

White may never have seen Chapman's *Warning* but he knew the artist's mural of *The Baptism of*

this cycle, for it inspired him to create works based on two of its themes. In 1852-53 he produced *The Requiem of De Soto* and *The Separation of the Pilgrims at Delft Haven.* White's rendition of the "warning" was most probably also executed during this period.

White's dramatically lit protagonist—like Chapman's—is given center stage and becomes the focus of the viewer's attention. The design of her deerskin clothing does not derive from the sixteenth-century drawings made at Roanoke Island; according to those images, the garment would not have been worn over both arms. But the idea of incised decoration was based on fact, as was the concept of draping a mantle over one shoulder alone. Characteristic of a Düsseldorf-style painting, additional details that might have proved distracting are hidden in darkness; the setting is subordinate to the action. Yet within the reduced light there are passages with varied shapes, colors, and textures. These are handled by White with notable skill.

To appreciate fully the renderings by Chapman and White, one must know more of the story behind the images. In the winter of 1608-9 the settlement at Jamestown was near starvation. The colonists' own

19

Figure 16 ❋ *Edwin White,* POCAHONTAS INFORMING JOHN SMITH OF A CONSPIRACY OF THE INDIANS, *c. 1850, oil on canvas 44 x 36 in. Courtesy of Mr. and Mrs. William Maury Hill, photograph by Katherine Wetzel.*

meager supplies were exhausted, and relations with tribes of the Powhatan confederation had so deteriorated that trading for food was no longer possible. In desperation, John Smith decided "to surprise Powhatan" and take his provisions, but others at Jamestown were reluctant. In late December, however, Powhatan "invited [Smith] to come unto him," to build for the ruler an English-style house, and to trade for a shipload of corn. Smith set out for Werowocomoco with a party of forty-six men.[38]

The "kind King" of the tribe at Warraskoyack on the James River warned Smith that Powhatan had "sent for you onely to cut your throats." The captain no doubt believed this warning, for he had come to suspect that Powhatan had killed the Roanoke Island colonists. From Warraskoyack he sent a soldier "to seeke for the lost company of Sir Walter Raleighs." Powhatan, for his part, after a year and a half of observation, had realized that the English were more than temporary visitors. At Werowocomoco he accused Smith of "comming hither . . . not for trade, but to invade my people, and possesse my Country."[39] The king apparently came to the conclusion that genocide would be a practical solution to his problem. Rightly, the two leaders suspected one another of the worst behavior and intentions. Their relationship, formerly hopeful when Smith believed the Indians to be intimidatable and Powhatan saw the English as a useful temporary ally, had deteriorated to distrust and treachery.

Powhatan then departed the village, accompanied by many of his women and children. He left a group of warriors with "a plot to have murdered Smith." The captain, however, escaped the ensuing confrontation, but, unable to retreat to his ship, which sat at low tide on the icy river, returned to "our old quarter." Powhatan then prepared a second attack on Smith by making "ready his forces to surprise the house and him at supper." At this point, Pocahontas, who was among those who had moved from the village to the woods with her father, intervened:

> Pocahontas his dearest jewell and daughter, in that darke night came through the irksome woods, and told our Captain . . . [that] Powhatan . . . would . . . come kill us all, if they that brought it could not kill us with our owne weapons when we were at supper. Therefore if we would live shee wished us presently to bee gone. Such things as shee delighted in, he would have given her: but with teares running downe her cheekes, shee said shee durst not be seene to have any: for if Powhatan should know it, she were but dead, and so shee ranne away by her selfe as she came.

When dinner was brought, Smith made the Indian servers "taste every dish." He then "spent the night as vigilantly as they, till it was high-water." At this point he returned to his ship and sailed away.[40]

As an epilogue to the story of the "warning" at Werowocomoco, the men Smith had left behind at Jamestown took to their own devices. Their desperate circumstances inspired them to mount their own expedition, which ultimately ended in disaster—the sinking of a boat and the loss of its crew in freezing water. "To advise the President [Smith] of this heavie newes," a volunteer, Richard Wyffin, set out for Werowocomoco. Not finding Smith there, "he did assure himself some mischiefe was intended." Wyffin was in dangerous circumstances, but in his hour of need a familiar savior appeared:

> Pocahontas hid him for a time, and sent them who pursued him the cleane contrary way to seeke him; but by her meanes and [by the] extraordinary bribes [made by Wyffin] and much trouble in three dayes travell, at length he found [Smith].[41]

If the rescue of Smith from clubbing and her warning of the captain about the dinner conspiracy were the first two "rescues" by Pocahontas, Richard Wyffin's salvation was the third. A fourth rescue of an Englishman took place shortly after Smith departed from Virginia in October 1609. The Indians, "no sooner understood Smith was gone, but they all revolted, and did spoile and murther all they encountered." Thirty of their victims were Jamestown settlers

attempting to trade with Powhatan. In that climate, "Pokahontas the Kings daughter saved a boy called Henry Spilman [Spelman], that lived many yeeres after, by her meanes, amongst the Patawomekes." Spelman, then fourteen years of age, eventually died at the hands of the Indians in 1623.[42] These third and fourth "rescues," which are not known to have been depicted by any artist, point to the English belief in the benevolence of the daughter of Powhatan.

THE ABDUCTION OF POCAHONTAS

DATE: April 1613

PLACE: Village of the Patowomecks on the Potomac River

RECORDED: Letter of Samuel Argall (1613); Ralph Hamor's *True Discourse* (1615); John Smith's *Generall Historie* (1624); letter of John Chamberlain (1613)[43]

The abduction of Pocahontas was of great interest to the editors of de Bry's *America* series. They recognized the importance of an incident that was interpreted in London as news that a colony "almost at the last cast" was suddenly doing "well." Some Londoners even speculated that Powhatan would thereby "bring them where they shall meet with gold mines."[44] As with the de Bry scene of the rescue of John Smith, the engraving of this incident is broken into a depiction of successive events, as described in contemporary sources ✳ (fig. 17).

The captor of Pocahontas was Captain Samuel Argall, a navigator and administrator who arrived in

Figure 17 ✳ *Unknown artist,* IAPASSUS PERSUADES POCAHONTAS TO VISIT SAMUEL ARGALL'S SHIP, *c. 1634, engraving, 5 ¾ x 6 ¾ in., published in the de Bry family,* America, *10. Virginia Historical Society, photograph by Katherine Wetzel.*

the colony in 1612 and was soon trading for corn with the Patowomeck Indians of what is now northern Virginia. In the spring of 1613, while Pocahontas was visiting that tribe, Argall's new friends relayed this news. He then returned, "resolving to possess my selfe of her by any stratagem that I could use, for the ransoming of so many Englishmen as were prisoners with Powhatan: as also to get . . . armes and tooles . . . [and] some quantitie of Corne, for the colonies reliefe." Argall went to a lesser chief of that region, Japazaws (Iapassus), and "told him, that if he did not betray Pokohuntis into my hands; we would be no longer brothers nor friends." For his efforts, Japazaws was promised a "small Copper kettle, and som other les valuable toyes."[45]

In the foreground of the engraving is depicted the persuasion of Pocahontas. Japazaws caused his wife to "faine a great and longing desire to goe aboorde, and see [Argall's] ship"; Japazaws refused to allow her to do so "without the company of women"; his wife then persuaded Pocahontas to accompany her. In the middle ground is portrayed the payoff to her betrayers, which is being concluded as Pocahontas makes her way toward the ship. The concluding scene is the shipboard supper, which was

there was to perswade her to be patient," as if to emphasize Argall's kind treatment of his kidnap victim.[46]

In the background are scenes of various forms of skirmishing, including the burning of a village. Such hostilities were typical of English-Powhatan relations in the years after Smith's departure and before the capture of Pocahontas. Indeed, these troubles are presented as justification for the abduction—the pirating of Pocahontas was acceptable because it would bring an end to warfare.

Powhatan was "much grieved" to learn of the capture of Pocahontas. He immediately sent instructions that the English should "use his Daughter well, and bring my [Argall's] ship into his River, and there he would give mee my demands." Argall, however, with Pocahontas on board, "repayred with all speed [to Jamestown] to Sir T[homas] Gates, to know of him upon what condition he would conclude this peace, and what he would demand."[47]

The arrival at Jamestown is depicted in a canvas of c. 1910 by Jean Leon Gerome Ferris, a prolific history painter of scenes of drama and romance taken from the nation's colonial and Indian past ✳ (fig. 18). In bold, colorful conceptions, Ferris delighted his colonial revival audience with imagery marked by pag-

Figure 18 ✳ *Jean Leon Gerome Ferris,* THE ABDUCTION OF POCAHONTAS, *c. 1910, oil on canvas, 24 x 35 in., Courtesy of William E. Ryder, photograph by Katherine Wetzel.*

"merry on all hands." All slept on board the ship that night, and in the morning Argall told Pocahontas he would "reserve" her as ransom. At this turn of events she "began to be exceeding pensive, and discontented." Ralph Hamor commented that "much a doe

eantry, affluence, and—in most instances—the noblest behavior. In his portrayal of this scene, the stately figure on the right, who presumably is Governor Sir Thomas Gates, embodies the dignity and virtue of Anglo-Saxon culture. A gracious, "innocent"

Pocahontas is obliged to recount to her dumfounded audience the treacherous behavior of Captain Argall, who stands to her right. In his notes about this painting, Ferris describes Argall as a "freebooter" (a plunderer or pirate);[48] the artist casts him as a foil against the other protagonists, who are seen as virtuous representatives of two great cultures suddenly brought together. The majesty and scale of Argall's ship, the lure of colorful costumes, and the interaction between disparate cultures beckon the viewer to imagine an appealing time and place that was the stage for such memorable historical events.

The saga of her kidnapping continued even after Argall's return to Jamestown. Within a "few dayes" Powhatan returned seven English hostages and three tools. This was not enough to satisfy either Gates or Sir Thomas Dale, however, and a year went by before another attempt was made to resolve this impasse. In March 1614, Dale with a force of 150 men, set out with Pocahontas toward Powhatan's residence. They were determined "either to move [the Indians] to fight for her . . . or to restore the residue of our demands."[49] A second de Bry engraving, which depicts the captive Pocahontas being visited on this journey by her brothers, illustrates the series of events that follows, as recorded in contemporary accounts ❋ (fig. 19).

The party traveled to Mattkot (Matchot), a village on the Pamunkey River sixty miles west of

Figure 19 ❋ *Unknown artist,* POCAHONTAS VISITED BY HER BROTHERS, *c. 1634, engraving, 5 ⅝ x 7 ½ in., published in the de Bry family,* America, *10. Virginia Historical Society, photograph by Katherine Wetzel.*

Jamestown and northeast of the present site of Richmond. There the river narrows to virtually a channel, and the forest grows close to its banks, but such facts were unknown to the de Bry artist. He portrays at the top right a village inspired by John White's depictions of settlements in the vicinity of Roanoke Island. In the middle ground is depicted an incident of taunting by the Indians. The English saw "about foure hundred

men well appointed" who "dared us to come on shore, which wee did." The Powhatans offered "no shew of feare . . . nor offered to resist our landing" but "walk[ed] boldly up and downe amongst us."[50]

A battle seemed imminent until the episode depicted in the right foreground unfolded:

> [T]wo of Powhatans sonnes being very desirous to see their sister who was there present ashore with us, came unto us, at the sight of whom, and her well fare, whom they suspected to be worse intreated, though they had often heard the contrary, they much rejoyced, and promised that they would undoubtedly perswade their father to redeeme her, and to conclude a firme peace forever with us.[51]

At about this point, however, John Rolfe announced to Dale by letter his love for Pocahontas and interest in marrying her. Dale readily approved the pairing, and thereby ended any chance for the "redemption" of Pocahontas, who by this time had already been baptized, or was in the process of becoming well versed enough in the religion of her captors to contemplate conversion.

THE BAPTISM OF POCAHONTAS

DATE: Late 1613 or early 1614 (after the capture of Pocahontas in April 1613 but before her wedding in April 1614)

PLACE: Either Henrico or Jamestown

RECORDED: Letters of Sir Thomas Dale, Alexander Whitaker, and John Rolfe, all appended to Ralph Hamor's *True Discourse* (1615); John Smith's *Generall Historie* (1624)[52]

In 1836 Virginian John Gadsby Chapman received a highly sought-after commission to paint one of four historical murals that would fill the long-vacant panels in the rotunda of the Capitol. Not only was such a commission the most prestigious that the nation could offer, but it also carried the sizable stipend of $10,000. The young painter was awarded this task largely through the efforts of his friend and former roommate, Virginia congressman Henry Wise.[53]

Chapman's effort, *The Baptism of Pocahontas*, is largely imaginary ❋ (fig. 20). It had to be because no details of this event were recorded. Even the location—Henrico or Jamestown—is uncertain because Pocahontas could have spent the year of her captivity at either or both locations. Sir Thomas Dale, the figure with whom she is most closely linked after her kidnapping, spent part of his time at Jamestown and part at Henrico, the town he had established in 1611 near the falls of the James River, and which he had autocratically controlled since. (This location, which is

Figure 20 ✳ *John Gadsby Chapman*, THE BAPTISM OF POCAHONTAS, *1836-40, oil on canvas, 144 x 216 in., U.S. Capitol Rotunda. Courtesy of the Architect of the Capitol.*

twenty miles below Richmond in Chesterfield County, is now referred to as the Henricus site.)

Dale was probably present at the baptism of Pocahontas because he claimed credit for her conversion: "Powhatans daughter I caused to be carefull instructed in Christian Religion, who . . . was, as she desired, baptised. . . . Were it but the gayning of this one soule, I will thinke my time, toile, and present stay well spent."[54] Chapman placed Dale (the figure in armor) in the left foreground of his mural.

John Rolfe, the twenty-eight year old widower who ultimately married Pocahontas, must certainly have been a prominent witness to her baptism. He too apparently played a major role in her conversion. John Smith recorded that by Rolfe's "diligent care" Pocahontas was taught to speak English "as might well bee understood," and was "well instructed in Christianitie."[55] Indeed, Rolfe stated that one of the reasons that he wished to marry Pocahontas was the opportunity it would provide to help assure her salvation. Chapman situates Rolfe in the right foreground, behind the kneeling convert.

If the baptism took place at Henrico, then Alexander Whitaker was most probably the Anglican

24

to achieve a level of historical accuracy for his painting, however. If a description did not exist, he would study objects and general records of the period and deduce what the scene must have looked like. Immediately after receiving his commission he sailed for England in search of authentic portraits of the key figures, of models for the costumes and furniture of the period, and for a church in which his baptism scene could took place. If he found no such portraits, at least Chapman uncovered in England paraphernalia of the sort that might have surrounded the figures, such as the green velvet chair that he found at Knole, which he sketched ✳ (fig. 21).[58] He later looked in Virginia as well for images of Pocahontas and Rolfe, but found none to his liking. However, he did acquire a painting by his friend Charles Bird King of Hayne Hudjihini, the young wife of Oto chief Shaumonehusse. Her image probably served as one of the inspirations for Chapman's Pocahontas.[59]

The artist also delved into the historical literature. Chapman discovered a number of primary documents, which he used in a pamphlet published to explain the reasoning behind his representation. Chapman provided a host of contemporary citations that account for the martial attire of Dale and the accoutrements of some of the other figures, explained the regulations of the colony that obliged colonists to attend church wearing their arms but forced Indians to abandon theirs, and discussed his choices concerning such objects as the chair and table near Dale, the font, and the pulpit, with its cloth and hourglass. He also identifies a number of the historical personages in the mural, including the first couple married in the colony (John and Ann Laydon), the first gentlewoman there (Mrs. Forrest), and two of the Englishmen saved by Pocahontas (Henry Spelman and Richard Wyffin).[60]

On two major points, however, Chapman took large liberties. First, wherever in Virginia the baptism took place, it would have been held in a church that was small, built of wood, and designed with little architectural distinction. Chapman's monumental edifice perhaps suggests his attempt to impart the proper dignity to the ceremony being described.

Second, Ralph Hamor recorded that two of Powhatan's sons and an uncle of Pocahontas were present at her wedding but says nothing about their presence at the baptism, an event perhaps less likely to have won the favor of her family. Chapman had no basis for including any Indians other than Pocahontas, but, because the problematic relationship between Anglo-

Figure 21 ✳ *John Gadsby Chapman,* CHAIR OF RAISED VELVET IN THE CARTOON GALLERY AT KNOLE, *early 1830s, pen and ink on tracing paper, 9 ¾ x 7 ½ in. Courtesy of the Valentine Museum, Richmond, Virginia, photograph by Katherine Wetzel.*

clergyman who administered the rites.[56] He had traveled to Virginia with Dale in 1611 and established himself as a missionary on the colony's frontier. Because Whitaker proudly related to a London correspondent that Pocahontas "openly renounced her countrey Idolatry, confessed the faith of Jesus Christ, and was baptised," some chroniclers of this moment, including Chapman, have incorrectly assumed that he was the minister at Jamestown.[57] There was no need for Whitaker at the original settlement, however, because Richard Buck was already in attendance there.

There is no additional information to be found in the documents that record the conversion of "Pocahontas" to "Rebecca." Chapman was determined

Americans and Indians was one of the crucial themes of his work, other native figures had to be included.

It is not surprising that Chapman had chosen a scene from Virginia history to fulfill his commission; he had long been interested in the history of his home state, and especially in the Pocahontas story. In addition, some Virginians during this period saw the need to respond to certain New Englanders who maintained that their "Pilgrim" forefathers had established the intellectual and moral foundations of the American republic, while the South had contributed virtually nothing of value, and, in slavery, much that was harmful. By depicting a scene from the story of Pocahontas, Chapman could remind visitors to the nation's Capitol that Virginia's history was actually older than that of New England, and no less vital to the establishment of the United States.

Also, by portraying this incident Chapman could give the Virginia founders credit for their own, rarely acknowledged, missionary errand. The artist was quick to point out in his pamphlet that the Jamestown colonists did not "exterminate the ancient proprietors of the soil, and usurp their possessions." Rather, they spread "the blessings of Christianity among the heathen savages." The story of the baptism of Pocahontas, he argued, "appeals to our religious as well as our patriotic sympathies, and is equally associated with the rise and progress of the Christian church, as with the political destinies of the United States."[61] For an age that, at least in theory, saw the continuing domination of North America as a Christianizing as well as a civilizing process, Chapman's theme should have struck a responsive chord.

The four principal figures in the painting are united by the intense color of their white, black, and red clothing, which sets them apart from the contingent of Indian figures to the right, on whom the light is less directly focused. Locked visually within the English group, and posed like traditional depictions of the Virgin Mary, Pocahontas seems already absorbed into English culture and religion and thereby free of the Indian civilization to which she has turned her back.

The Indians who view this ceremony seem to be divided in their reactions. Pocahontas's uncle, at the far right, and her seated sister with the infant child, watch and placidly accept her conversion. Two others apparently do not. The morose seated Indian is, according to the pamphlet, Opechancanough, Powhatan's brother, "the sullen, cunning, yet daring" chief who had captured John Smith in 1607 and would lead a massacre of the English in 1622. Chapman imagined that at the baptism Opechancanough "probably even then brooded over" his plan of hostility. The standing, resplendent Indian figure is Pocahontas's brother Nantequaus. Chapman reprints Smith's description of him as "the manliest, comeliest, boldest

26

spirit I ever saw in a Salvage."[62] He, however, looks away from the conversion of his sister, as if he cannot bear to witness her transformation.

The official pamphlet emphasizes that some Indians are ungovernable and must therefore be treated with force and removed. Chapman's depiction of Opechancanough as a potential troublemaker provided a historical precedent for, and a confirmation of, the theory behind the Indian Removal Act of 1830. This bill provided for the relocation of many eastern tribes to lands in the still undeveloped Louisiana Purchase. Chapman's mural suggests that Indians who cooperate by abandoning their own beliefs and adopting the culture of the Europeans might be allowed to assimilate and, by surrounding his unarmed Indians with armed Englishmen, makes clear what will happen to those who do not.[63]

Smith's account of the "diligent care" given by Rolfe to Pocahontas during the process of her cultural appropriation[64] may have been the inspiration for a depiction of this subject by James William Glass, a history and portrait painter whose promising career was cut short by his suicide in New York City in 1855 ✳ (fig. 22). Glass no doubt conceived this painting to supplement Chapman's mural by providing an earlier, foundational event. His figures are cruder than those of Chapman but bear a noticeable resemblance to them. Rolfe, who was aware that the "education [of Pocahontas was] rude [and] her manners barbarous," said that as a tutor he was encouraged throughout by her "desire to be taught and instructed in the knowledge of God, [and] her capableness of understanding."[65] Glass, however, saw more than a teacher-student relationship in their sessions. Rolfe embraces Pocahontas, and neither's eyes are directed at the crucifix to which he gestures.

Pocahontas must surely have pondered the choice between what Thomas Dale termed "her countrey['s] Idolatry" and "her Christian faith."[66] About 1854, in a clear attempt to follow the mid-century vogue of such American sculptors as Randolph Rogers and Erastus Dow Palmer to provide Christian America with suitable biblical figures and religious themes, Joseph Mozier carved in marble an image of a young Pocahontas in deliberation ✳ (fig. 23). If this work is not notable in terms of its aesthetics, as Nathaniel Hawthorne stated when he recalled his visit to Mozier's workshop, it did perhaps serve to remind the artist's contemporaries of the primacy of their reli-

Figure 22 ✳ *J. W. Glass,* JOHN ROLFE AND POCAHONTAS, *early 1850s, oil on canvas, 35 x 26 in. Virginia Historical Society, photograph by Katherine Wetzel.*

gion.[67] When this sculpture stood in his studio in Rome, in the shadow of the Vatican, the crucifix that she holds must have seemed as plausible as the deer at her side. No doubt some saw Mozier's Pocahontas as a prefiguration of later representations of the simple peasants of nineteenth-century Italy, whose closeness to nature seemed to make them closer to God. Such rustics became popular subjects for romantic artists.

This sculpture probably served as well to provoke thoughts about the extraordinary nature of this Indian girl. She is somehow aware that a conversion to the strange religion of the European newcomers is in her future. Romantic viewers inclined to ponder the early history of America might then remember that her powers as a visionary were also evidenced in her rescue of John Smith, which symbolically allowed for the providentially favored Anglo-American race to begin its domination of North America.[68]

THE WEDDING OF POCAHONTAS

DATE: April 1614

PLACE: Jamestown, or possibly Henrico

RECORDED: Ralph Hamor's *True Discourse* (1615), including letters by Sir Thomas Dale, Alexander Whitaker, and John Rolfe; John Smith's *Generall Historie* (1624); William Strachey's *Historie of Travaile into Virginia Britannia* (after 1611)[69]

Henry Brueckner's celebratory painting of the wedding of Pocahontas, which is nearly six feet long, served as the model for a large, popular engraving ✳ (fig. 24). Brueckner himself worked primarily as a printmaker, and so he no doubt conceived his image with a print in mind. Through that medium it became widely known. The print was engraved by John McRae and published by Joseph Laing, who at mid-century began distributing large-scale prints out of his shops in New York, London, and Edinburgh. Laing produced engravings of a number of history paintings, including the four new murals in the United States Capitol, one of which was Chapman's *Baptism of Pocahontas.* Among the other romantic subjects he offered was a pair that represented two crucial moments in the life of the "Father" of the nation: *The Prayer at Valley Forge* and *Father, I Cannot Tell a Lie.* All of Laing's pieces were described in booklets printed to advertise the sale of such engravings.

Unlike Chapman's mural of Pocahontas's baptism, Brueckner's

Figure 23 ✳ *Joseph Mozier,* POCAHONTAS, *modeled c. 1854 (this version inscribed on its base "187"— the last digit has not been carved), marble, 48 ½ x 19 x 16 ⅞ in. Courtesy of the Chrysler Museum, Norfolk, Virginia; gift of James H. Ricau and Museum Purchase, photograph by Scott Wolff.*

wedding scene carries no statements about southern
pride or government policy toward Indians. To be
sure, any work about Pocahontas would have been of
particular interest to patriotic Virginians, among whom
were a number of budding sectionalists, but this scene
had a more universal appeal and was distributed to audiences in both the North and South, as well as in Europe. In one respect, however, the baptism and wedding paintings are similar. Brueckner's scene is also
largely imaginary, but in this case the creative imagination was as much that of Chapman as Brueckner, because his wedding scene essentially duplicates much
from the earlier composition. Few details of the marriage ceremony were recorded, and Brueckner probably felt safer following Chapman's basic approach
than he would have had he felt the need to work out
his idea from scratch.

What is perhaps best known from the documentary record of the marriage of Pocahontas are the sentiments of the bridegroom. During Pocahontas's captivity, "John Rolfe had bin in love with [her] and she with
him." Although his "hartie and best thoughts [had] a
long time bin so intangled," Rolfe was hesitant to pursue
marriage. A union with the immediate family of
Powhatan would hold enormous political implications.
Thus Rolfe sought the "grave and mature judgement" of
Sir Thomas Dale "either [to] perswad[e] me to desist, or

incourag[e] me to persist therein." In the same long letter Rolfe agonized over what he perceived to be a moral
dilemma. He attempted to convince himself that he was
not motivated by "the unbridled desire of carnall affec-
tion" but was acting "for the good of this plantation, for
the honour of our countrie, for the glory of God, for my
owne saluation, and for the converting to the true
knowledge of God and Jesus Christ, an unbeleeving
creature, namely Pokahuntas." Rolfe concluded that
marriage to Pocahontas would be morally correct, even
a "holy . . . worke." How could he "refuse to leade the
blind into the right way"? How could he not "give bread
to the hungrie" or "cover the naked"? How could he fail
to "actuate these pious duties of a Christian"?[70]

This letter caused some debate about whether
Pocahontas's baptism or marriage came first. Rolfe
seems to be arguing that their union would help to bring
her to Christianity. It is almost certain, however, that
the settlers would have held to the canonically correct
baptism-marriage order, and so we might suspect that
Rolfe was using the theological argument as an attempt
to justify his more carnal and political intentions.

Perhaps because he had been recently freed from
the burden of his deliberations, Rolfe is portrayed by
Brueckner as a buoyant figure at the time of his marriage. His statements to Dale provide a historical basis
for the enthusiasm depicted here, which was also noted

28

in the pamphlet that was published to market the engraving.[71] Its author, historian Benson J. Lossing, imagined Rolfe at his wedding to be the "personification of manly beauty in form and carriage." Pocahontas is envisioned as thoroughly domesticated and Anglicized; she would thereby have been more appealing to Victorian viewers than a generic Indian girl. Lossing describes her as the embodiment of "womanly modesty."[72] Brueckner's Pocahontas was clearly not meant to remind viewers of the impulsive, spirited young woman who had dared to intercede between the powerful leaders of two cultures.

As at the baptism, Thomas Dale would almost certainly have been present at the wedding. A religious zealot and autocrat, he had sanctioned the marriage as being "for the good of the Plantation" and "another knot to binde this peace the stronger."[73] Brueckner, like Chapman, places Dale on the left side of the composition and even seats him in Chapman's chair. If the wedding took place at Jamestown, Richard Buck would have officiated. Lossing, however, identifies Brueckner's minister as Alexander Whitaker, who presided at Henrico, but who was included in Chapman's baptism scene.

The presence of at least three Indians at the marriage ceremony is documented. When Powhatan was told of the proposed marriage of his daughter, he found it "acceptable" and gave "his sudden consent thereunto." "Some ten daies after [Powhatan] sent an olde uncle of hirs, named Opachisco, to give her as his deputy in the Church, and two of his sonnes to see the marriage solemnized." In Brueckner's image, the uncle is the adult Indian seated at the right, next to a younger brother of Pocahontas. An older, taller brother is pictured standing behind John Rolfe. All are shown giving attentive approval to the proceedings. Brueckner's interpretation is based on a contemporary account that after the marriage the English enjoyed "friendly commerce and trade, not onely with Powhatan himselfe, but also with his subjects round about us."[74] There is no documentary basis for the Indian bridesmaids and attendants the artist introduced.

Brueckner and Lossing concluded that "all then at Jamestown [must have been] present at the marriage." On that basis the artist felt justified in increasing his congregation. Lossing matches names to a chart of the scene that he offers in his booklet. Some well-known figures, such as Henry Spelman, the boy (and now young man) Pocahontas had saved, are in attendance, but other personages, like Mrs. Edward Easton and her child, the Thomas Powell family, or Mrs. Horton and her grandchild, have little interest for the viewer. They are present to give the illusion of historical accuracy, but the numerous errors made by Brueckner and Lossing undercut this intention. For instance, Sir Thomas Gates, who is shown seated beside Opachisco, had already returned to England by the time of the wedding; George Percy, who is identified as the figure standing beside the older brother of Pocahontas, had not been in the colony since 1612; and Mrs. John Rolfe and child, who are shown directly beneath the minister, were deceased. Indeed, her death had freed Rolfe to marry Pocahontas.[75]

The setting for the marriage would have been a small, undistinguished structure of wood, but Brueckner places it in a Chapman-like architectural fantasy. Seizing on one of the few facts recorded about this event—that the marriage took place "about the fi[r]st of April"—Brueckner draped his building with Virginia flora. Lossing imagines "the fragrance of the wild flowers," which are woven into the "festoons of evergreens and sprays" that fill Brueckner's interior. Lossing expands on the artist's depiction, digressing about spring in Virginia, when "the trees are robed in gay and fragrant blossoms," when "the robin, the blue-bird, and the oriole" give "concerts in the woods," and the communion table can carry "bread from the wheat fields of Jamestown, and wine from its luscious grapes."[76] In fact, the English settlers grew little wheat and grapes. Be that as it may, if print buyers wanted evidence of a joyous, festive event, Brueckner and Lossing spared little in providing it for them.

POCAHONTAS IN ENGLAND

DATE: 1616-17

PLACES: Plymouth, London, Brentford, Gravesend

RECORDED: Letters of John Chamberlain (1617); Samuel Purchas's *Purchas His Pilgrimes* (c. 1619); John Smith's *Generall Historie* (1624)[77]

Pocahontas's journey to England was an arrangement of the Virginia Company, the organization that sponsored the Jamestown settlement. While the company was continually in search of investors and colonists and eager for the potential financial rewards of colonization, its leadership also had a genuine concern that Virginia's Indians be Christianized. Pocahontas, the converted daughter of a chief, was impressive evidence of the attractiveness of Virginia as an investment and of the founding's success as a missionary endeavor. The civilized, charming, and apparently intelligent Pocahontas was the antithesis of the majority of the natives in the de Bry volumes, many of whom were portrayed as savage beings who routinely practiced murder and cannibalism. She embodied the potential of the Virginia venture, and the company wanted to show her off. The reception provided for "Rebecca Rolfe" was warm, and her visit generated a great deal of attention and excitement.

Pocahontas, Rolfe, and Thomas, their son of less than two years, left Virginia in the spring of 1616 with

Sir Thomas Dale and his party. Also on this voyage was Uttamatomakkin, Powhatan's priestly adviser, who was sent to investigate the homeland of the English. His presentation at court is firmly documented; Uttamatomakkin afterward stated his displeasure concerning a king "who gave me nothing."[78] Pocahontas may not have been present on this occasion, but there can be no doubt that both Americans attended an important theatrical performance. "The Vision of Delight" was a Twelfth Night masque that was staged by Ben Jonson in January, 1617. John Chamberlain reported that "the Virginian woman Poca-huntas, with her father counsaillor [Uttamatomakkin] hath ben with the King, and graciously used, and both she and her assistant well placed at the maske."[79] However, the popular story that James I was annoyed with Rolfe for having the audacity to marry a "princess" was actually invented by Robert Beverley at the beginning of the eighteenth century.[80]

Throughout the months of Pocahontas's stay in London, the Virginia Company provided her with a small living allowance and saw to it that she was presented to English society. John Smith records that Thomas West, baron De La Warr, the former governor of the Virginia colony, and his wife assisted with the introductions. No doubt Thomas and Elizabeth Dale also saw to it that she was made known to, and when possible exhibited for, those whom the Virginia Company hoped would become or remain patrons. Samuel Purchas documented his impressions of Pocahontas and mentioned one of these arranged meetings:

> And his [Rolfe's] wife did not onely accustome her selfe to civilitie, but still carried her selfe as the Daughter of a King, and was accordingly respected, not onely by the Company, which allowed provision for her selfe and her sonne, but of divers particular persons of Honor, in their hopefull zeale by her to advance Christianitie. I was present, when my Honorable & Reverend Patron, the L[ord] Bishop of London, Doctor King entertained her with festivall state and pompe, beyond what I have seene in his great hospitalitie afforded to other Ladies.[81]

The Virginia Company ultimately voted the sum of £100 to the Rolfes "to set forward the busines of bulding a Colledg in Virginia for the trayneing up of those heathen Children in true religion."[82]

Even Chamberlain, a disgruntled investor in the Virginia Company who disparagingly referred to "the Virginia woman" as "no fayre Lady," bore witness to the quality of her reception: "With her tricking up and high stile and titles you might thincke her and her worshipfull husband to be sombody [of distinction]." The Rolfe family preserved as relics of this period a pair of earrings and two buttons reputed to have been

worn by the princess while she was in England ❋ (fig. 25). All no doubt were made in the Old World; no jeweler in America would demonstrate such craftsmanship for decades. These pieces, however, came

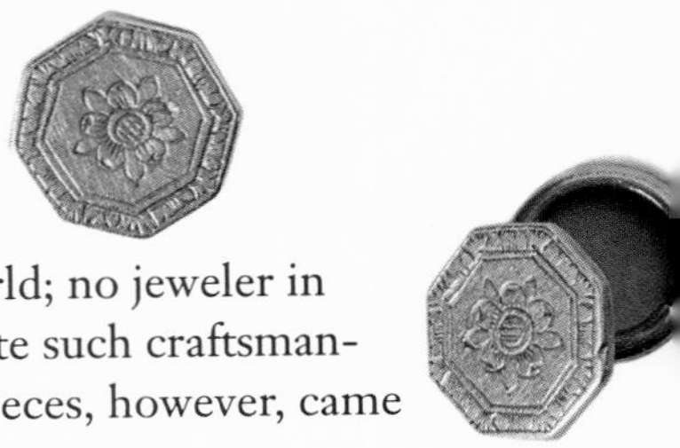

Figure 25 ❋ BUTTONS, *date unknown, gold, ¼ in. diameter. Virginia Historical Society, photograph by Katherine Wetzel.*

into institutional collections in the mid-twentieth century with virtually no documentation.[83]

When John Smith left the Virginia colony in October 1609, he vanished from Pocahontas's life for some seven years. (She apparently had been told that he was dead.) Although Smith asserted he had "introduced" Pocahontas to Anne of Denmark in a 1616 letter that outlined her accomplishments and aid to the Jamestown settlers, this text did not appear until the *Generall Historie* of 1624, and so there is some doubt as to its authenticity as an introduction. After "reproducing" this letter, Smith described a meeting between Pocahontas and himself at Brentwood, outside of London in Middlesex. There the princess reproached the captain for his less than courteous treatment of someone who had done so much for him: "After a modest salutation, without any word, she turned about, obscured her face, as not seeming well contented; and in that humour . . . we all left her two or three houres. . . . But not long after, she began to talke, and remembered mee well what courtesies shee had done." Pocahontas demanded from Smith a reaffirmation of their special bond of friendship: "You called [Powhatan] father being in his land a stranger, and by the same reason so must I doe you." Smith's report of this encounter, which surprisingly indicts his own behavior toward this American "princess," also calls attention to his failed relations with the English nobility.[84]

The Rolfes began the return trip to Virginia in the early spring of 1617 but got no further than Gravesend. There Pocahontas died, the victim of an illness that had "unexpectedly" developed. Her Christian faith remained constant; those who witnessed her death were "joy[ous] . . . to heare and see her make so religious and godly an end."[85]

Following her burial, in March 1617, John Rolfe returned to Virginia, leaving Thomas in the care of his uncle. Thomas Rolfe returned to Virginia as an adult and settled first in Surry County and then in what is now the Hopewell area. This return occurred, however, long after his father had died, during and possibly as a direct result of the uprising of 1622, which was led by Opechancanough, his mother's uncle.

The Christian aspect of the death of Pocahontas interested Junius Brutus Stearns, an accomplished antebellum history painter, whose depictions of the life of George Washington include a similar scene of a physical death met with steadfast conviction. His *Death of Pocahontas* ✳ (fig. 26) presents a fully Anglicized figure who had been transformed from her savage origins and thereby made worthy of Christian salvation. He recreates on canvas the denouement of this exemplary story. If the baptism of Pocahontas was an important event in American history (and American history painting), Stearns provides the necessary conclusion to this narrative of conversion.

Stearns's stunning reconstruction of a scene for which no record survives is a remarkable display of history painting. He conceives a setting that is believable as provincial England. He paints muted paneled walls as a foil for lush fabrics that call to mind her social achievement. He juxtaposes English and Indian figures to suggest the bringing together of cultures that was the meaningful accomplishment of Pocahontas. Her youthful appearance, her beauty, and the distraught postures of her husband and son establish the pathos of the event. The painting on the wall, appropriately, is a mourning scene.

In the latter part of 1616 Pocahontas was sketched by Simon van de Passe for an engraving that was commissioned to present an image of the Virginia Company's honored guest to the largest possible audience. As we shall see, it was from this representation that one of the two dominant schools of Pocahontas portraiture emerged.

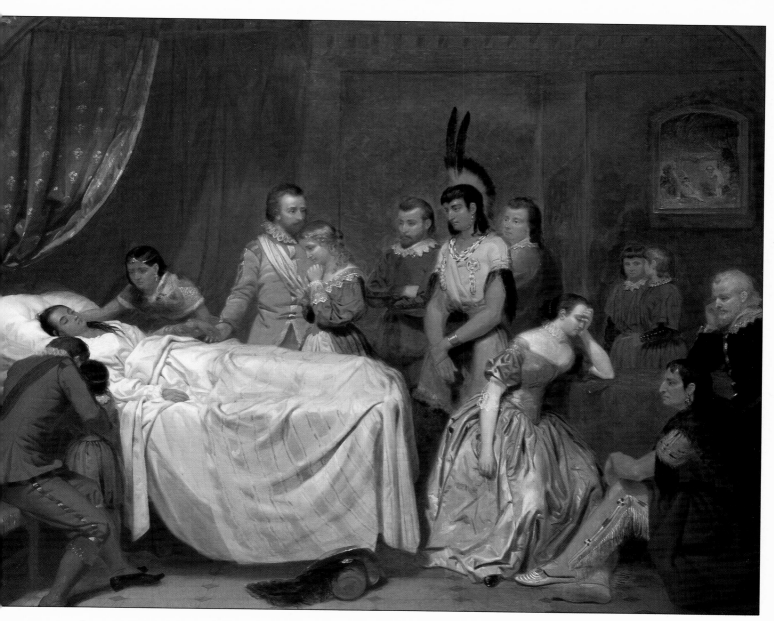

Figure 26 ✳ *Junius Brutus Stearns,* THE DEATH OF POCAHONTAS, *c. 1850, oil on canvas, 36 x 42 in. Courtesy of Nicolas Windisch-Graetz.*

The Legend of
POCAHONTAS

3

The Portraits after
Simon van de Passe

The best estimate of the true appearance of Pocahontas can be drawn from Simon van de Passe's engraving ✳ (fig. 5). He also provides the crucial information that she was twenty-one years old in 1616 (the same age as the artist). Van de Passe, one of the sons of the important Elizabethan engraver Crispin van de Passe the elder, was a competent artist. He had been born in Cologne and had traveled to London in 1613 in hopes of following in his father's footsteps as a portraitist to the English court.

Against a rigid, rather masculine costume, "Matoaka als [as] Rebecca" seems stiff and uncomfortable. She wears a high neckline that may have seemed unbecoming at the time for so young a woman although not inappropriate for a mother. It gave the chaste image the Virginia Company no doubt wanted to project, and it very probably hid tattooing that would have troubled if not appalled Jacobean eyes. She holds an ostrich feather, which had long been a symbol of royalty. Beyond the apparent attempt by her sponsors to Anglicize Matoaka into Rebecca by means of a European costume, the artist provides what seems to be a truthful record. The heavy, slightly dark, and handsome features of a Powhatan Indian are visible. Van de Passe does not attempt to make his sitter beautiful in a sense that would have appealed to English eyes. He gives us instead the woman who caused acquaintances of John Smith to remark only that they had "seen many English Ladies worse favoured, proportioned and behavioured."[86] It is this truthfulness that apparently incited later efforts to correct the perhaps overly honest attempt by van de Passe to capture an actual appearance.

Almost two centuries later, the van de Passe engraving was reissued in London by W. Richardson ✳ (fig. 27). In this work of 1793, her costume remains virtually the same, but her features have become

more those of an Englishwoman. To eighteenth-century European eyes, this less "native" Pocahontas perhaps came closer to achieving the beauty that would have been expected of the "Indian princess" of legend.

Figure 27 ✳ *Unknown English artist (after Simon van de Passe),* POCAHONTAS, *1793, engraving, 7 1/4 x 5 in., published by W. Richardson. Virginia Historical Society, photograph by Katherine Wetzel.*

32

The so-called Booton Hall portrait of Pocahontas is also derived from the van de Passe engraving ✷ (fig. 28). (For many years the reverse was thought to be true.) It is a loose copy, imprecise in details of costume and insensitive to the subject's Indian

Mɑtoɑks aℓs Rebecka daughter to the mighty Prince Powhatan Emperour of Attanoughkomouck aℓs Virginia converted and baptized in the Christian faith, and Wife to the Worℓℓ Mʳ Tho: Rolff.

Ætatis suæ 21. Aº.1616.

Figure 28 ✷ *Unknown English artist (after Simon van de Passe),* POCAHONTAS *(Booton Hall portrait), probably eighteenth century, oil on canvas, 31 x 24 in. Courtesy of the National Portrait Gallery, Smithsonian Institution.*

features. The colors are remarkably inaccurate: the sitter's dark skin and black hair are Europeanized to be white and brown, and even her white beaver hat is mistakenly made black. The unknown artist did produce a portrait of a beautiful young woman, however, and thereby inspired the theory that the van de Passe engraving was simply a poor copy of this attractive work. Inadvertently, Thomas Rolfe's name was inserted on the canvas in place of John, which argues for a posthumous date, because a contemporary artist would certainly have been aware of her husband's correct name. Indeed, the provenance of the painting would seem to date it no earlier than the second half of the eighteenth century. This painting, however, as testified by its in-

clusion in the Columbian Exposition in Chicago in 1893, was apparently thought of at the end of the nineteenth century as the most accurate depiction of Pocahontas.

If the Booton Hall portrait added color to the original engraving, Richard Norris Brooke, about 1905, enlarged it to full-length and presented the new image on a monumental scale, literally as large as life ✷ (fig. 29). A Virginia portraitist and history painter who lived alternately in the northern part of the state and the nation's capital, Brooke took obvious pride in the accomplishments of Virginia's favorite daughter. The viewer sees her as she might have appeared standing across the room at a London social event. No longer is Rebecca Rolfe poorly "favoured, proportioned and behavioured." Instead, this idealized Pocahontas is physically attractive. With hands on her hips and a leg thrust forward, she throws back her masculine costume with the spirit and energy of a saucy young woman who knows her beauty. Brooke's Pocahontas would certainly have attracted male eyes in the England of James I, and perhaps suggested the connection between her own sensuality and the intoxicating product that she was, at least in part, being used to advertise.

A final attempt to represent Pocahontas, which, while it stands alone, at least derives from an English tradition of painting, is an oil executed by a Boston schoolgirl named Mary Woodbury during the 1730s ✷ (fig. 30). It is a rare painted image from colonial America of a historical figure, and it probably owes its existence to a book, Robert Beverley's *History and Present State of Virginia.* First published in 1705, a new edition appeared in 1734 and seems to have been advertised that year in the *Boston Gazette* by means of an anonymous letter to the paper, which described Pocahontas as embodying "virtue," and "greatness of Mind," and "all that can be lovely or great in a Female Character."[87] There is no evidence that Woodbury saw the letter or that the painting even postdates it, but clearly the letter and the painting document a shared perception. Woodbury's primitive and charming image bears little resemblance to the historical figure and is instead a colonial girl's conception of an ideal woman. The deportment, elegant dress, and flower all are standard elements of formal English portrait painting of

Figure 29 ✳
Richard Norris Brooke,
POCAHONTAS,
c. 1905, oil on canvas,
84 x 52 in. Courtesy of
the Virginia Museum
of Fine Arts, Richmond;
gift of John Barton
Payne, photograph by
Ron Jennings.

Figure 30 ❋ *Mary Woodbury,* POCAHONTAS, *c. 1730, oil on paper, 15 ¼ x 12 ½ in. Courtesy of the Massachusetts Historical Society.*

as best he could and apparently made a faithful copy. What survived of the original portrait disappeared a decade or two later, but in 1842 Daniel Rice and James Clark produced in Philadelphia a large color lithograph of Sully's copy ❋ (fig. 31). Their image appeared in Thomas McKenney and James Hall's three-volume collection, *The History of the Indian Tribes of North America*, which was published between 1836 and 1844. The image in the print differs slightly in its various editions. In at least one version her hair is somewhat tangled; in all, Pocahontas is a short, stocky figure. In 1838 John Gadsby Chapman saw the Robert Matthew Sully copy from which the print derives and called the figure "coarse and unpoetical."[89] Compared to his own later efforts, and to the elegant portrait by Thomas Sully, the Pocahontas of the Turkey Island portrait is precisely that.

Both Robert Matthew Sully and McKenney and Hall mistakenly thought that the Turkey Island portrait was taken from life. Although it was certainly an old painting, it did not date from 1616, for the style of the costume worn by Pocahontas did not exist before the second half of the seventeenth century. The late seventeenth- or early eighteenth-century portraitist

the Georgian period as it was exported to the American colonies. Mary Woodbury may not have been influenced by the van de Passe engraving, and she had no way to know that her work would predict, in some respects, a second tradition of Pocahontas portraiture, the Turkey Island portraits.

The Turkey Island Portrait

The story of the Turkey Island portrait goes back at least to the second half of the eighteenth century.[88] At that time, Ryland Randolph (1734-1784), the son of Richard Randolph and Jane Bolling Randolph, and therefore, through his mother, the great-great-grandson of Pocahontas, acquired during a visit to Warwickshire, England a pair of portraits said to represent his most famous ancestor and John Rolfe. These paintings, which were owned by Rolfe descendants, were given to Randolph when he asked to buy them. He brought the portraits back to his Virginia residence, the James River ancestral home of the Randolphs, Turkey Island.

Early in the nineteenth century, portraitist Thomas Sully saw the Turkey Island portraits. In 1830, from faraway Philadelphia, he urged his nephew Robert Matthew Sully, a resident of Richmond, to copy the image of Pocahontas. The younger Sully found the painting literally in pieces. He put the parts together

Figure 31 ❋ *After the Turkey Island portrait,* POCAHONTAS. *1842, lithograph, 20 1/4 x 13 3/4 in., published by Daniel Rice and James Clark for Thomas McKenney and James Hall's* Indian Tribes of North America, *1842. Virginia Historical Society, photograph by Katherine Wetzel.*

borrowed some features from the van de Passe engraving (which the latter work loosely resembles) or from a now lost portrait from life. The loose hair and costume were invented to provide an alternative image for Pocahontas, which was not so rigid, formal, and Europeanized as the van de Passe figure.

As soon as Robert Matthew Sully made public his copy of the Turkey Island portrait, a debate about the authenticity of the image raged across the pages of the Richmond *Enquirer*. In letters to the editor, as in the family correspondence of the Bollings (a prominent branch of Pocahontas's descendants in 1830), supporters and detractors of this rendering of the princess of Virginia took their stands. Although this controversy might have been a function of the fear of miscegenation in nineteenth-century America, because some family members might not have wanted to emphasize their mixed blood, this explanation is doubtful, because descendants of this particular interracial marriage had long been proud to claim their Indian ancestry. More likely, the detractors of the Turkey Island image simply believed that this stocky individual could not possibly be a true representation of the princess of Virginia.

William Bolling, who at one point had owned and abandoned the Turkey Island portrait, wrote that this image was not of Pocahontas, or, for that matter, of any other Indian: "it represented a large, fat, sallow [person of] rather a dead white skin, enormously large breasts much exposed, brown curly hair with *blue* Eyes." Bolling was proud to have earlier talked Charles Willson Peale out of making a copy of it. His solution to the debate was a public referendum: "Let's hang [it] up . . . in a public room in Richmond and let the people judge for themselves." Some of his relatives were quick to add their support. Linnaeus Bolling proclaimed that Sully's "Dowdy, Gross, coarse & homely picture" must not be forced on the family as a likeness of Pocahontas, who would have been a "delicate, slender, & beautiful young Girl."[90] John Gadsby Chapman thanked William Bolling for relieving him of the burden of using this figure as the model for the Pocahontas of his *Baptism*, adding that an "ill favored" image of her could "break the beau ideal . . . and romance of her story."[91]

Other relatives, however, flatly disagreed. The oldest living descendant of Pocahontas, David Meade Randolph, a brother-in-law of William Bolling and the executor of the estate of Ryland Randolph, remembered the paintings being brought over from England. Edward Lynch remarked that William Bolling's daughter was the very counterpart of Sully's copy.[92]

Robert Matthew Sully was undeterred by the controversy over the Turkey Island portrait. He held, in his copy, what he believed to be the one true image of the American heroine, and he continued to be drawn to the romance of her story. In 1855 he volunteered to

a potential patron that "she has been the idol, of my romantic dreams, from boyhood!" Sully did, however, think that the costume of the Turkey Island portrait was "absurd," not because he recognized its style as of a later period, but because with it "all Indian association was destroyed." His solution to that problem was to rework the image in a "more ideal style, more in accordance with Indian character."[93] He was the first portraitist to present the Pocahontas of the years before 1613, before her absorption into English culture. This new effort, which was painted in the early 1850s, was given to the Virginia Historical Society by the artist ❋ (fig. 32).

Sully had read in Robert Beverley's *History and Present State of Virginia* that Powhatan girls would dance "crowned with a wreath of flowers." Using that passage as his inspiration, the artist decided to "represent a beautiful girl, nude to a little below the shoulders, so as to preserve [a] perfect delicate association, . . . the only approach to costume, the fur of some animal." The fur is historically accurate, he argued, as are the wild flowers, which are "beautiful & *poetic*" as well. He goes on, "My *effort was* to preserve the likeness, contour, feature of the *copy* (my copy) from the *preserved* original," yet "change the *civilized*, or rather *fashionable*, Princess, to the beautiful *forest girl*, of more *pleasant association*—The Guardian Angel of the Colony!"[94]

Sully "preserved" the original less than he professed, for his figure, to use his word, is "beautiful" and idealized to appeal to nineteenth-century Anglo-Saxon eyes. The descendants of Pocahontas no doubt approved of this new, more charming image. At least, William Maxwell, president of the Virginia Historical Society in the 1850s, told Sully he was "much pleased with [the] design; as agreeing with his *ideal*, completely."[95] This "guardian angel," however, was far removed from Sully's first copy.

Sully's figure of the forest was linked in his own mind with the hero of many of the nineteenth-century novels and dramas about the Virginia founding, Captain John Smith. The artist imagined "many wild scenes of romantic adventure" with the "chivalrous" Smith and "the darling Princess" Pocahontas "hand in hand." He regretted Smith's "not marrying that dear Girl!" "Then the romance would have been *perfect* instead of its 'lame & impotent conclusion,' " he wrote in 1854. "That she loved him is evident!"[96]

Sully described his "forest girl" as the complement to the other Pocahontas, the "civilized . . . Princess." To his thinking, the Turkey Island image was not regal enough. He thought that he could paint a better portrait of this second persona of Pocahontas, and later he did so ❋ (fig. 33). Sully presents Pocahontas with a crown, and in garments of regal

Figure 32 ✳ Robert Matthew Sully, POCAHONTAS, *early 1850s, oil on canvas, 36 x 29 in. Virginia Historical Society, photograph by Katherine Wetzel.*

century portraits, which tended to show less and less concern for historical authenticity, had in effect "caught up" with the idealized images of the "rescue," which showed little allegiance to the bare historical narrative reported by Smith.

Other than the likeness by van de Passe, the Thomas Sully portrait of Pocahontas is perhaps the best-known representation of the princess ✳ (fig. 34). The elder Sully was conscious of the brewing sectionalism on both sides of the Mason-Dixon line, and after completing his portrait in 1852, he immediately donated it to the Virginia Historical Society, perhaps as a way of winning new friends and patrons in her home state. Sully devised the sort of image that would please Virginians. His Pocahontas is notable for her handsome, if somewhat Mediterranean, features, which are far removed from both the Roanoke Island natives depicted by John White and the van de Passe "Rebecca." This Pocahontas also presents herself, through her obvious grooming and deportment, as a person of remarkable refinement and grace. The clothing is English, if stylistically inaccurate, and the setting is a mountainous Virginia landscape, although the landscape she would have known would have been flat. Such "problems," however, would have been ignored by Sully's audience. In perhaps the most technically superior of the portraits based on the Turkey Island model, Sully here gives us Pocahontas at what might have been construed as her best moment—after her absorption into English culture but before her fateful trip to England.

Yet this image too had its contemporary detractors. John Esten Cooke, a future Confederate general who ultimately had more to say about Pocahontas and her narrative, chastised portraitists of both traditions. They had, he argued, "made either a fat Spanish woman, or a dame of the court of king James the first, in a hideous ruffle, and farthingale and hat, of my fairy of the days of romance."[97] It is perhaps safe to say that by the second half of the nineteenth century Pocahontas had become a figure of the mind's eye, and that any artist would encounter problems in an attempt to capture her myriad qualities.

colors, red and green. This Pocahontas is a gentle, amiable girl who is totally a figure of fantasy. She wears the clothing of a European princess, which suggests a conception about royalty that had no counterpart in the Powhatan political system. This image continued the process of pushing the limits of delineations of Pocahontas and her narrative. Such mid-

Pocahontas and Sectionalism

Long before the sectionalists carried their differences to the battlefields of the Civil War, northern writers and historians had seized on the Pocahontas narrative as both a vehicle and a target. As the progenitrix of many slave-holding planters, as well as of some of the most ancient families of the Old Dominion, Pocahontas was seen as the figurative mother of the antebellum Virginia aristocracy. Northern historians rightly believed that she was venerated in the South and therefore lampooned her and her story, while certain abolitionist propagandists found in the Pocahontas narrative a means to attack slavery and thereby attempt to undercut the economic basis of the states that would become the Confederacy.

As early as 1820 "Pocahontas" was used as a pseudonym, in part because she symbolized safety for the endangered captive and the possible peaceful co-existence of two distinct races, but also because this "princess of Virginia" had herself been a partner in a "mixed marriage" and therefore was perhaps not the best representative for a culture whose self-definition was based on racial separation.[98] For instance, the satirical, antislavery pamphlet *Pocahontas; A Proclamation* presented the Virginia aristocracy as believing in its own right to slaves and in the ultimate domination of the free states by the "Lordly lions of the South." In

Figure 34 ✳
Thomas Sully,
POCAHONTAS, *1852,*
oil on canvas, 36 x 28 in.
Virginia Historical Society,
photograph by
Katherine Wetzel.

Emily Clemens Pearson's abolitionist novel of 1852, *Cousin Franck's Household,* the story is told through the letters of "Pocahontas," a young white woman from Connecticut who travels to the Virginia plantation of her relations and is horrified by the barbarity of this system.[99]

Indeed, it was partly because of Pocahontas, and her provision of an alternative history for the South through her actions and a completely southern aristocracy through her numerous, often affluent descendants, that the people of the slave-holding states were able to begin to think of themselves as a confederacy. Her story gave southerners a common historical point of origin and a common heroine, and therefore it is not

surprising that in the years leading up to the Civil War it came under attack. New England historians attempted to discredit the South's efforts to formulate and maintain a distinct cultural identity by undercutting the historicity of the rescue of John Smith. That episode, however, although it did provide fodder for debate, was by the outbreak of the war far too deeply ingrained in the national consciousness to be affected by such attempts to undermine it.

John Esten Cooke, in his poem of January 1861, "A Dream of the Cavaliers," invoked the great figures of Virginia's past in an effort to instill pride and patriotism in the young men of the South, who within months would be firing shots in anger at their northern

39

brethren. Chief among these were "the Knight of the Virgin Queen," John Smith, and "the Virgin Queen of the West," Pocahontas. In these identifications we see Smith represented as a soldier of Elizabeth I, the original "Virgin Queen" who had much to do with the establishment of the British empire, and Pocahontas as the New World version, whose actions began the chain of events that allowed for the formulation of the American empire, and by extension, the entity that would soon be known as the Confederate States of America. Cooke believed that the courage of such figures as Smith and Pocahontas should be remembered in the hard times ahead.[100]

In 1860 a militia unit that would become Company E of the 4th Virginia Cavalry carried the inspiration of Pocahontas with them on a ceremonial flag ❋ (fig. 35).[101] They called themselves the "Guard of the Daughters of Powhatan," in part after their home county, which is situated just west of Richmond on the James River. When the unit was organized, the women of the county presented to their defenders the ceremonial flag on which was pictured the most famous daughter of the leader after whom their county was named. The guard's banner was woven of yellow silk, overpainted in oil by an unidentified hand. On the reverse was the Virginia state seal.

The figure on the flag is derived from Thomas Sully's portrait and easily recognizable as Pocahontas. She wears a crucifix, which seems to identify her as the post-baptism Rebecca, who had found the religion and culture of English Virginia superior to that she had known before. Further, the antebellum women of Powhatan County, the "daughters" whom the guard would be defending, saw themselves as

Figure 35 ❋ *Unknown artist,* BANNER OF THE POWHATAN GUARDS, *1860, silk with oil painted seal, 35 x 40 in. Courtesy of the Museum of the Confederacy, Richmond, photograph by Katherine Wetzel.*

figurative (and in some cases literal) descendants of that Christian heroine and mother of the Virginia aristocracy. It would have been an honor for those daughters to have been associated with the most famous daughter of Virginia.

The soldiers who followed this image would be inspired to display the courage that had been exhibited by Pocahontas during a potentially life-threatening crisis. Similarly, there was apparently a sense that the sailors on ships christened with the names of famous, and often long-dead, Indian leaders and tribes might show some of the fearlessness, dignity, and, when necessary, savagery that had come to be associated with Indian warriors. A ship with an Indian name, which sported an Indian figurehead, could also have been immediately identified as American and so might have signaled safe haven for citizens of the United States in all parts of the world.

Arguably the most important ship in the United States Navy at the outbreak of the Civil War was the *Powhatan*, which since its commissioning in the early 1850s had served the nation valiantly. The *Powhatan* was Commodore Matthew C. Perry's flagship on one of his trips to Japan, had fought against Chinese pirates, and had protected American interests in Mexico, before being called back to the east coast when hostilities looked imminent. Neither the *Powhatan*, nor its subordinate vessel, the *Pocahontas*, arrived soon enough to relieve Fort Sumter, but each was involved in later engagements in the War between the States. The irony of ships named *Pocahontas* and *Powhatan* using their guns against the sons of Virginia would probably have been obvious to those fighting on both sides of the line.[102]

Because Pocahontas was known to have taken a long voyage to England from which she never returned, it was an appropriate and romantic notion for a ship with her name to roam the Atlantic Ocean and her figurehead to plow its waves. There were a number of ships named *Pocahontas* afloat during the antebellum era, including several transports and whalers. The carved figurehead shown ❊ (fig. 36) is a depiction of Pocahontas, which once adorned a merchant ship or whaler owned by the wealthy Philadelphian Stephen Girard. His profile portrait is said to be the likeness on the medallion that she holds. (An alternate interpretation makes this figure her fellow Virginian George Washington.) According to tradition, when this ship was retired, the figurehead was transformed into a cigar-store Indian by the additions of a crown of feathers and the leaves of tobacco that she holds, a story that seems to be borne out by a close examination of this figure. This sculpture has been repaired many times, and its original surface has been lost

to twentieth-century repainting.[103]

If the carving of this sculpture lacks some of the assuredness and style of the hand of William Rush, the highly accomplished artist to whom it had been attributed, it remains a striking work despite its altered condition. Indeed, it is one of the more spectacular of early nineteenth-century American ship carvings to survive. The stance and attitude of the figure not only suggest Rush or a carver working under his influence but also closely resemble—except for the plunging neckline—the well-known sculptures by Rush of *Peace* and *Virtue*. Such qualities would certainly have been identified with Pocahontas, although it must be admitted that the features of this figure are not those of an Indian, nor is her nineteenth-century dress appropriate. Such problems suggest that the figure may not originally have depicted Pocahontas.

Figure 36 ❊ *Unidentified artist*, FIGUREHEAD OF POCAHONTAS, *c. 1820-30, pine, polychrome, 33 ½ x 23 x 33 in. Courtesy of the Kendall Whaling Museum, Sharon, Massachusetts.*

Pocahontas and the New Virginia

The debate between sectionalist propagandists over the veracity of the rescue of John Smith raged long after the cessation of violent hostilities. During the post-war period, however, Pocahontas remained a popular figure in her home state. In 1885 John Esten Cooke wrote perhaps the best novel about the princess, *My Lady Pokahontas*. In this account Cooke alternately defended the great events of her life and provided various imaginative subplots, including her previously unknown crossing of paths with Shakespeare at a performance of *The Tempest*, where the playwright admits that many of the experiences of Miranda are based on those of the American princess.[104] In 1887 Wyndham Robertson expanded on his earlier efforts in an attempt to provide a complete genealogy of her family. And

41

William Wirt Henry was still writing articles defending the rescue of John Smith as late as the 1890s.[105]

If the Civil War did not initially change the perception that Virginians held about Pocahontas, however, it did so eventually, in an unexpected way. The very foundation of southern society was shaken by the war, emancipation, and Reconstruction. One way that some Virginia traditionalists fought back was to become intensely racist. That turn of events bode nearly as much ill for Indians—and therefore for the memory of Pocahontas—as it did for the newly liberated blacks.

Concurrently, the end of the nineteenth century brought new demands for scientific studies of the native cultures. The emphasis should be on truth, scientists insisted, rather than romantic legends. Adolphe Bandelier, an anthropologist and colleague of the great Lewis Henry Morgan, called for the destruction of "Cooper's Indian braves," "Princess Pocahontases," and all other sentimental and fictional representations that tended to cloud the minds of the public and made them unprepared for scientifically derived truth.[106] Contemporary interpreters of the Pocahontas narrative, however, entirely ignored such pleas. Instead, they invented new and surprisingly diverse readings of the story.

In 1907, the three hundredth anniversary of both the founding of the Jamestown colony and of the settling of the North American continent by the English, a tercentennial exposition was staged at Norfolk, near the site of the original landing. This exposition was modeled after the great American fetes of the previous century, including the 1876 Philadelphia Centennial and the 1893 Columbian Exposition in Chicago. Collier's magazine devoted the cover and two feature articles to the fair in its issue of 27 April 1907. Artist J. C. Leyendecker was commissioned to paint the cover ✳(fig. 37).

If Leyendecker envisioned the drama and spectacle of the encounter between two proud cultures, which marked the beginning of the American nation, he painted an odd, apparently awkward first meeting. Though the Indian depicted is not specifically identified, she is clearly Pocahontas, who by this time was the Indian most closely associated with this event. The only other figure from the Jamestown founding then generally known was John Smith, who is almost certainly represented as the cavalier who so gallantly introduces himself. The image is outlandish for a number of reasons, not the least of which is that the commoner John Smith wears the silver pointed star of the Order of the Garter, the highest caste of English knighthood.

Figure 37 ✳ *J. C. Leyendecker,* JAMESTOWN 1607, *1907, oil on canvas, 26 x 19 in. Courtesy of American Illustrators Gallery, New York, and Harry and Connie Lockwood's Midwestern Galleries, Cincinnati, Ohio.*

Although Leyendecker was producing this image for popular consumption, there is evidence to show that the story of the Jamestown colony, other than the names of its marquee figures, had by this point slipped the minds of many Americans. Virginia congressmen

42

who lobbied for federal funding to support the tercentennial found colleagues in the House of Representatives who had never heard of the town. Perhaps for that reason, President Theodore Roosevelt decreed that the fair would not recreate the Jamestown settlement and a Powhatan village but would be "an International Naval, Marine, and Military Celebration." There would be a dramatic juxtaposition between two eras, rather than two cultures. Roosevelt's celebration of American progress would parade American battleships in waters where a Spanish threat loomed three centuries ago and, one could argue, had recently returned. In his speech at the opening festivities, Roosevelt had not a word to say about Pocahontas or John Smith, nor did the text of the *Collier's* article that outlined the Norfolk exposition. Events had transpired in Virginia that greatly complicated the view that even the most patriotic citizens of the Old Dominion had for their formerly favorite daughter.

Pocahontas was also virtually ignored in the second *Collier's* article, which was titled "Jamestown and What Happened There." Although one might have assumed that this implied northern authorship, the writer was in fact Thomas Nelson Page, a Virginian, who in novels, short stories, and essays had for decades eloquently lauded the virtues of the antebellum culture of his home state. To the reader of Virginia history during this period, however, most of the points that he made would have been predictable: the first English settlement was at Jamestown, not in New England; the Virginia colony, rather than that of the Puritans, "more than any other contributed to the making of this Republic"; and Virginia had produced a number of men of "genius" and "character," such as George Washington, John Marshall, James Madison, Robert E. Lee, and Stonewall Jackson.

Page used the word "savage" to describe the Powhatan Indians and mentioned Pocahontas only as the savior of Smith, whom he saw as the important figure in the Jamestown story. The two illustrations that surrounded Page's text show an Indian with bow and arrow in hand, about to shoot a cavalier. The contrast between that imagery and the *Collier's* cover is as different as the northern and Virginian interpretations of the significance of the history that unfolded at Jamestown.

A sculpture of John Smith was commissioned at the time of the Jamestown anniversary, and one of Pocahontas was planned as well. A national Pocahontas Memorial Association was incorporated for that purpose in 1906, but sixteen years elapsed before William Ordway Partridge's bronze, life-size statue of the princess was unveiled on Jamestown Island ❋ (fig. 38). Partridge saw Pocahontas not as a savage who in-

Figure 38 ❋ *William Ordway Partridge*, POCAHONTAS, *1906, bronze, 88 x 42 x 33 in. Courtesy of the Association for the Preservation of Virginia Antiquities.*

43

tervened providentially into Anglo-Saxon history but as a person of exceptional virtue and a peacemaker. That was the Pocahontas described as well by Lyon G. Tyler, who in 1914 at the dedication of a plaque to her in the church at Jamestown described a woman of "splendid moral force and purity of purpose," who "hated war and loved peace and truth and saw no reason whatever why the sons and daughters of men whether white or red or yellow or black might not dwell on this earth in amity and peace forever."[107]

Drawing in part on his background as an actor, Partridge presents a figure whose dramatic, theatrical stance effectively suggests her passionate concern to spare bloodshed. The impression is that Pocahontas has emerged from the woods and is walking into the Jamestown village again, as she did four centuries ago. She comes with seriousness and sincerity, and she gestures in peace. It matters little that the figure is a woman of perhaps eighteen or twenty years instead of the girl of twelve to fourteen who visited the settlers when John Smith was there. Nor is it a concern that she wears clothing more befitting a western Indian than a Powhatan, or that the peculiar sandals on her feet would have been as unknown to her culture as would the almost Art Nouveau floral design incised on her vest, both of which are visually appealing if inaccurate. What is significant is that Partridge answered well his commission to create a monument that halts the viewer and inspires remembrance of Pocahontas and her accomplishment. When the sculpture was unveiled in 1922, Mrs. John Lightfoot, the chairman of the Jamestown committee of the Association for the Preservation of Virginia Antiquities (APVA), which owns the Jamestown site where Partridge's statue stands, saw the statue's "crowning beauty" to be "its radiant womanliness with its impulse of interest and love that pervades its every aspect."[108] Few tourists on Jamestown Island today walk past the monument without pausing to look at it.

Perhaps surprisingly, only half of the $10,000 awarded to Partridge for the commission was raised by 1912;[109] the remainder was not forthcoming for more than a decade. If we can judge by this failure to support the monument, something had happened in Virginia to make more complex the reputation of the figure described in 1835 as the "tutelary deity" of the state.[110]

Following the near overthrow of the old order, many Virginians had become so traditionalist and racist that they were no longer sure of what they thought about Pocahontas. In the new Virginia, Pocahontas had two strikes against her: she was an Indian and an independent woman. As an Indian, she was retroactively grouped by the Anglo-Saxon majority in the same category with blacks and immigrants, who threatened order and racial integrity. White Virginia extremists during the early 1920s formed the Anglo-Saxon Clubs of America (1922) and forced passage of a law designed to thwart miscegenation and harass racial minorities (1924). This law defined a white as "a person who has no trace whatsoever of any blood other than Caucasian." There was one exception, however. In a complexly worded passage, the descendants of Pocahontas, who were too prominent to offend even in this climate, were exempted from the strictures of the law by a corollary termed the "Pocahontas Exception," which stated that those with one-sixteenth Indian blood would also be deemed white persons.[111]

The "modern" woman who had acted with an independence unknown to the Victorian era could also be associated with a second threat of undesired change. This is exemplified by the denunciation of the "Gibson Girl," a representation contrived by Charles Dana Gibson, by Sara Rice Pryor, another APVA leader. The "Gibson Girl" was not only beautiful and dignified, fashionably clothed and groomed, but also active and independent of old strictures. As a substitute model of female behavior Pryor offered Mary Ball Washington, whose biography she had written. Pryor admired the mother of the president for being "self-denying, diligent, and frugal."

In general, the APVA advocated the worship of historical figures whose model behavior would inspire virtuous action. The heroes they preferred were, for the most part, men. The few women who were recommended were not those who had crossed the boundaries of prescribed feminine behavior, as Pocahontas had done.[112] Further, Pryor thought that the Powhatan Indians "had not a single virtue or single trait of true nobility." Yet she proudly claimed Pocahontas as an ancestor, if only because she "conquered every instinct in her savage nature" and behaved "with discreet gravity." "Like the lovely pond lily, the root was in slime," Pryor wrote, "but at the first touch of the sun the golden heart was revealed of a perfect flower."[113] The "sun" here is clearly the English colonists, whose arrival precipitated the "budding" of Pocahontas.

In the context of Anglo-Saxon racism, Pocahontas did offer two virtues. By her baptism and absorption into English society, Pocahontas had admitted, even underscored, the superiority of that branch of European culture. Her actions in relief of Smith and Jamestown actually assured the Anglo-American domination of the continent. Another APVA leader, Cynthia Tucker Coleman, called Pocahontas a "divine" instrument who had been used to redeem America "from the dominion of the savage to yield its wealth of soil and climate to that race which should dominate the world."[114] In *Old Time Belles and Cavaliers*, published in 1912, Edith Sale argued that Pocahontas had more to do with the fate of the western continent than any woman except, perhaps, Isabella, the queen of Spain who sent Columbus on his way.[115] In the end, the tra-

44

ditionalists could only conclude that the preserver of the Jamestown settlement was an important historical figure who, if nothing else, at least warranted a statue.

If APVA members such as Sara Rice Pryor had detested the "Gibson Girl," they must have cared even less for the similar creation put forward by Howard Chandler Christy. His "Christy Girl" took the fashionable look and independent character of the "Gibson Girl" and replaced some of the dignity of the latter with an increase in youthful sensuousness. Christy defined his idealized "girl" as "high bred, aristocratic and dainty though not always silken-skirted; a woman with tremendous self-respect."[116] He saw Pocahontas as not only a "Christy Girl," but also as one of eight "Liberty Belles," famous females of American history who had prefigured the independent young women of his generation, and so had led to their "making" or evolution. He published a book about his "Liberty Belles" in 1912 and developed his image of Pocahontas into a six-foot oil painting ✳ (fig. 39).[117]

Although she looks English, Christy's Pocahontas seems by no means ready for absorption into English

Figure 39 ✳ Howard Chandler Christy, POCAHONTAS, 1911, oil on canvas, 69 x 49 in. Courtesy of American Illustrators Gallery, New York.

45

culture, by either conversion or marriage. No crucifix hangs at the end of the prominent necklace she wears, and she is clearly resisting, and perhaps disdainful of, her English suitor. Just as Daphne, in classical mythology, fled the love of Apollo, Christy's Pocahontas could not return the apparent love of her pursuer because to do so would cost this independent young woman her freedom, a valued characteristic of the "Christy Girl." There is no resolution to this problem. Daphne transformed herself into a tree to avoid Apollo; Christy's Pocahontas seems nearly ready to do the same.

Sara Rice Pryor and Howard Chandler Christy offered extreme interpretations of what Pocahontas had come to signify in the Virginia and America of the early twentieth century. Pryor had made clear her distaste for the Indian past of Virginia yet had attempted to maintain her connection to the most important figure of that past, who at least exemplified for her the ability to rise above unfortunate circumstances and exhibit appropriate behavior. Christy, a renegade illustrator who made few excursions into the past, used the Pocahontas story to elucidate a contemporary phenomenon of feminine behavior and fashion, which admittedly he had helped to define. Each in her or his own way, however, emphasized the freedom from a "primitive" past that one can read into Pocahontas's assertive, apparently pro-English actions.

A more traditional illustrator, Jean Leon Gerome Ferris, who has already been mentioned for his depiction of the abduction of Pocahontas ✳ (fig. 18), painted a portrait of Pocahontas about 1921 that offers an opposing view ✳ (fig. 40). He had looked at the van de Passe engraving and found the "thoughtfulness in its glance" so compelling that he decided to develop the image further. Ferris savored history and tried to recreate it, while adding as much romanticism as necessary to give his scenes interest. He imagined for himself and for his viewers how famous events must have seemed to those present, and he took it on himself to evaluate the

lives of famous people. He concluded that Pocahontas had led a life that not only was brief but must also have been unfulfilled: "Poor Pocahontas! A short life, and we fear not a merry one. Married to Rolfe, it is to be suspected . . . [that] she kept a savage's adoration for Captain John Smith." Instead of depicting a courtship

Figure 40 ✳ *Jean Leon Gerome Ferris,* MATOAX, *c. 1921, oil on canvas, 35 x 24 in. Courtesy of William E. Ryder.*

between the princess and the captain, as had some writers of the previous century, he shows its melancholy unfulfillment. By identifying the year as 1614 and inscribing the name "Rebecka" on the canvas, Ferris tells us his Pocahontas is baptized yet hesitant to take her assigned place in history. She still wears her Indian clothing, still retreats to the solace of nature, and presumably still dreams about John Smith. She apparently wants neither English culture nor the En-

46

glishman Rolfe but remembers instead a happier time when she could remain a Powhatan and Captain Smith was in Virginia. Ferris's forest setting at least seems plausible, if the clothing and sentiments he gives Pocahontas cannot be documented.[118]

A "Wanton Yong Girle"

William Strachey's *Historie of Travaile into Virginia Britannia*, which had been published in 1849, began to receive renewed attention during the early twentieth century. Literary figures such as Hart Crane and William Carlos Williams used Strachey's representation of the "wanton" adolescent who had cartwheeled naked with the boys of the settlement and who had been already married and divorced before her union with Rolfe to emphasize the physicality and sexual attractiveness of Pocahontas. In this tradition, Christy painted a version of the rescue in 1926 in which a bare-breasted, "Christy Girl" Pocahontas saves John Smith from his executioners.[119]

In the next decade, Paul Cadmus provided a sensual and athletic Pocahontas in his large mural commissioned by the Works Progress Administration for the Parcel Post Building in Richmond, Virginia ✳ (fig. 41). Pocahontas practically cartwheels into the scene. Her sensuality, however, is matched, and perhaps even exceeded, by that of Smith and the virile Indian men who are in various stages of undress. Following the vogue in the 1930s for "regionalist" art that looked to the American scene and to local themes in place of European modernist subject matter, Cadmus must have settled easily on this famous Virginia subject for a Richmond commission. The new valuation of Pocahontas as a sexual creature may have made her best known episode particularly appealing to him; at any rate he developed it into a powerful, almost monumental composition, made up of strong, anatomically precise figures with clear muscular definition. This mural, unfortunately, was removed when the postal facility was renovated in 1973, and the wall on which it hung was altered. The canvas is preserved by the federal government's General Services Administration, which plans to conserve the painting and reinstall it in the original building, now used for the GSA and court offices.[120]

Figure 41 ✳ *Paul Cadmus,* POCAHONTAS SAVING THE LIFE OF JOHN SMITH, *1938-39, oil and tempera on canvas, 82 x 162 in. Commissioned for the Parcel Post Building, Richmond.*

47

Epilogue

The Legend Today

One of the most powerful recent adaptations of the Pocahontas narrative is *Matowaka*, a portrait of her as a black woman ✳ (fig. 42). This image was contrived

Figure 42 ✳ *R. L. Morgan Monceaux,* MATOWAKA, *1993, pastel and mixed media, 41 x 31 in. Courtesy of Morgan Rank Gallery.*

in 1993 by R. L. Morgan Monceaux, a black, self-taught artist, who included it in his series of figures from the American frontier. His effort is clearly derived from the van de Passe engraving and is apparently the first ever to offer a black perspective on the Pocahontas story.

It has been noted that the Pocahontas legend was adapted by abolitionist writers who criticized Pocahontas's white, slave-holding descendants for hy-pocrisy. They gave the name Pocahontas to various protagonists to make the archaic nature of southern society apparent to their readers, but they were not so outlandish as to name one of the slaves Pocahontas, a ploy that might have underscored the inconsistency of the planter's racism while providing the reader with an interesting perspective on the position of the slave in antebellum Virginia. In a curious way, Monceaux's contemporary image recalls the distorted viewpoints of both the apologists for slavery who were proud of "Indian" ancestry and of the racist Virginians of the early 1920s, who in their 1924 miscegenation law lumped Indians and blacks together as "colored."

Precisely because Indians and blacks have shared a common ground in this culture and have both been represented and represented themselves as outside of the cultural mainstream, Monceaux is able to understand and depict what Pocahontas, who is pointedly referred to here by her more correct "Indian" name, might have experienced. Her story is similar to that suffered by many blacks. She too was kidnapped aboard a European ship and held against her will. English intruders imposed their "civilization" on both groups—the Indian nations whom they dispossessed of their lands, and the black populations, who were stolen from their homelands and forced into slavery. Both were, and often continue to be, forced to assume patterns of Anglo-Saxon culture in order to survive in America.

Using pastels and mixed media, Monceaux vigorously recycles the van de Passe portrait. By placing his black Pocahontas in the formal, rigid costume of the earlier image, he cleverly suggests the white cultural domination and containment of both peoples. He incorporates real lace as the only sensible way to match the inconceivable precision of lace in the van de Passe engraving, and his strong sense of linear design and color give a new boldness to the older, stiff image.

For Monceaux, ribbonlike lines of text are both a component of design and a source of information for the viewer. Their graffiti-like character translates the European decorum of van de Passe into a portrayal of the inner-city, street language of modern America. In this work they describe the various episodes of the Pocahontas narrative and offer at least two clues to the artist's viewpoint. On the one hand, when the English "resettle[d]" Virginia, they ignored the rights of the existing population of the region. One must also remember, however, that Matoaka was a "most remarkable person." She was to be admired for her bravery and for her accomplishments in so alien an environment.

For the past six years the Pocahontas legend has consumed the interest of Virginia artist Mary Ellen Howe, who has painted what is at this point the newest version of the van de Passe image ✳ (fig. 43). Reared in the state, Howe has known the Pocahontas legend all her life; she became intrigued by it when re-

Figure 43 ✳ *Mary Ellen Howe,* POCAHONTAS, *1994, oil over a photograph on tapestry-x paper, mounted on masonite, 24 x 20 in. Courtesy of Mary Ellen Howe, photograph by Katherine Wetzel.*

searching a book she published in 1984 about an eighteenth-century Virginian named Richard Bailey, who lived near the falls of the James River, where Pocahontas and her descendants had settled. As a portrait artist Howe knew that no painter ever had rendered an accurate image of Pocahontas, and she became driven to do correctly what the Booton Hall artist of the eighteenth century had failed to accomplish.

She would determine by every means possible the actual appearance of Powhatan's daughter and paint a color image that is as truthful as the van de Passe black-and-white engraving. She consulted art historians, costume historians, and a fabric manufacturer in this country and in England.

Howe gives us Pocahontas wearing the white beaver hat with white feather that van de Passe recorded, as well as an Indian's black hair and none of the lipstick and rouge invented by the artist of the Booton Hall portrait. By consulting archival photographs in the museum of the Pamunkey and Mattoponi Indians and taking her own snapshots of a young woman of the Rappahannock Indian tribe, Howe was able to estimate the probable skin color of Pocahontas. In the process of that research, the artist noticed in the facial structure of some modern Virginia Indians the same overbite, dimpled chin, and high cheek bones that van de Passe had seen in Pocahontas and repeated those features. She also kept from the engraving the patterns in the red patterned-silk coat of Pocahontas and the hand-stitched gold embroidery on the undercoat of what probably was gold brocade, details the Booton Hall artist had ignored. Howe has produced what is probably the most accurate portrait of Pocahontas that has been or can be painted. Asked why she undertook this painting, Howe explains that she could not forget a woman whose extraordinary accomplishments included the adoption of a foreign culture and the winning of acceptance by seventeenth-century English society.

The best-known twentieth-century adaptation of the Pocahontas narrative no doubt will be the full-length animated film produced by Walt Disney Studios and scheduled for release in 1995 ✳ (fig. 44). Disney's selection of the Pocahontas narrative is unexpected. The film's completion on the four hundredth anniversary of the birth of Pocahontas is coincidental. The subject was chosen as part of Disney's ongoing process to search out classic stories that can be retold through animation. In searching for a story from the lore of the better-known Plains Indians, the Disney staff decided instead on a life of Pocahontas because her legend—if not the culture of the Powhatan Indians—is well known and a great story. Also, her name itself, which already has recognition, holds resonance akin to that of Pinocchio or Snow White. Disney felt that its artists could integrate elements of fantasy and magic with the core legends and historical facts about Pocahontas and thereby bring her story to the screen as an animated film. It would present the Pocahontas story in a new way to a new audience around the world, yet be true to the spirit of her life and legend.

49

Disney was also interested in Pocahontas because her story lends itself to timeless themes that are especially relevant today. Because native Americans have for too long been ignored by Anglo-American historians, or at least unfavorably portrayed, the Disney film, which views the settlement of Jamestown from the perspective of the Powhatans, interprets their culture respectfully. The story of Pocahontas is told from the point of view of this maturing young woman, who faces momentous choices that will direct her life and the future of her nation. Her decisions, however, are not weighed in the context of the Anglo-American history of the United States. Rather, it is her attraction to the newcomers, which must be weighed against her allegiance to her family, her culture, and herself, that provides much of the dramatic tension in the film.

Pocahontas will also acclaim the American Indians' environmental awareness and understanding of the interrelationships between the land and the plant and animal worlds. Never before has the Pocahontas story been told with so much emphasis on its setting. The unknowing English want to plunder the land for its gold, and Pocahontas must explain to Smith that man cannot own land and therefore does not have the right to destroy the ground on which he stands. A raccoon braids her hair, the wind talks to her, and "grandmother tree" gives Pocahontas spiritual advice, but rather than have this imply an unsophisticated culture, we are left to ponder, with Pocahontas herself, which of these races are the true "savages." Nature and the natural are rendered in this film with gently bending ovals and circular lines of composition, which are interrupted by, and contrasted to, the angular triangles and rectangles of the English-made structures that intrude on the land.

Disney's *Pocahontas* ends in 1609, when John Smith departs Virginia. The film therefore celebrates only the early episodes of her life, when Pocahontas remained a Powhatan Indian. It avoids the later complications of her kidnapping, conversion, marriage, and untimely death. The crucial episodes of this period are recounted, however, in that she rescues Smith and saves the struggling Jamestown colony. Smith is shown to be younger and handsomer than his portrait from life, but this interpretation is perhaps truer to the twenty-seven-year-old adventurer who landed in Virginia in 1607. Pocahontas is made older than her thirteen years, but her appearance derives partly from that of a living Virginia Indian whom the Disney researchers interviewed. If some of the facts in this story are altered or embellished, the filmmakers are simply following the nineteenth-century tradition of making her story their own. The

Walt Disney film will again expand the Pocahontas legend and, by including new elements, will further obscure for the public the line where the primary sources end and fictionalization begins. But viewers of an animated film expect fantasy and may lump invented elements such as the Pocahontas-Smith romance with the fantasy of the "grandmother tree." In any case, the Disney film will succeed in bringing much of the history as we know it to the largest audience that ever has been exposed to her tale. And it will convey the essential element of the story—it will demonstrate that Pocahontas was an individual of unusual energy and vision who influenced the course of history.

From the time that Americans first looked to their heritage, they recalled the legend of Powhatan's

favorite daughter. The guises assigned to Pocahontas and her story have been of extraordinary variety and ironically often expressed antithetical viewpoints. She was remembered as a figure of refinement and grace, as both a "princess" and an "angel of the forest," while other representations of Pocahontas, which were thought to be "coarse and unpoetical," were rejected as simply untrue. Her legend was dragged into the feuding of the sectionalists, and Confederate soldiers paraded her image. American ships were identified with her name, and her memory was set adrift on the ocean she never recrossed. She has been called "the Virgin Queen of the West" as well as a "savage" of an inferior race. She was judged to be a humanitarian, a "champion of peace and truth," while contemporane-ously being incarnated as a self-focused "Christy Girl."

Our exhibition has touched on but a few of the adaptations of the Pocahontas story contrived by liter-ary and visual artists over the past four hundred years. These examples demonstrate the ongoing flexibility of her narrative. We now look ahead to Walt Disney Studio's version of her story, and beyond that to the four hundredth anniversary of the Jamestown founding in 2007, confident that artists from different eras and cultures will continue to invoke for their own purposes the woman whom poet Vachel Lindsay respectfully called "our Mother, Pocahontas."[121]

Figure 44 ❋ *Walt Disney Studios,* POCAHONTAS. *1994, iris print. Courtesy of The Walt Disney Company.*

Notes

William M. S. Rasmussen is Virginius C. Hall Curator of Art at the Virginia Historical Society

Robert S. Tilton teaches American literature at Queens College, City University of New York

Introduction

1 *Herman Melville*, The Confidence Man: His Masquerade *(Evanston and Chicago, 1984), p. 140.*

2 *One scholar who has discussed Pocahontas as Joan of Arc is Ann Uhry Abrams, in "The Pocahontas Paradox: Southern Pride, Yankee Voyeurism, Ethnic Identity, or Feminine Heroics," a paper delivered at the annual meeting of the American Studies Association, Miami, Fla., October 1988.*

3 *One French map, c. 1739 by Jean Baptiste Nolin, Jr., shows in a vignette the marriage of Pocahontas. It is owned by the Library of Congress and illustrated in Stuart E. Brown, Jr.,* Pocahontas *(Berryville, 1989), p. 21.*

4 *Bell Inn in London, owned by a proprietor named Savage, had been a residence of Pocahontas during her visit of 1616-17. A century later, Joseph Addison in one of his* Spectator *essays renamed it "La Belle Sauvage" ("The Beautiful Savage") in honor of her. He could think of a heroine born and nurtured in a natural environment only as a person of beauty. See* Pocahontas, La Belle Sauvage *(London, after 1956); this flyer discusses the bronze sculpture of Pocahontas by David McFall commissioned by Cassell Publishing House in 1956.*

5 *William Strachey,* The Historie of Travaile into Virginia Britannia, *Works issued by the Hakluyt Society, 1st ser., 6 (London, 1899), p. 111. See also Charles Edgar Gilliam, "His Dearest Daughter's Names,"* William and Mary Quarterly, *2d ser., 21 (1941): 239-42.*

6 *John Smith recorded that the "wit, and spirit" of Pocahontas were without parallel among her people (Philip L. Barbour, ed.,* The Complete Works of Captain John Smith (1580-1631) . . . *[3 vols.; Chapel Hill and London, 1986], 1:93, 274; 2:260. Those qualities apparently made her a favorite of the many children of her father Powhatan.*

7 *More in-depth discussions of many of these topics are provided in Robert S. Tilton,* Pocahontas: The Evolution of an American Narrative *(New York, 1994). See also William Warren Jenkins, "Three Centuries in the Development of the Pocahontas Story in American Literature" (Ph.D. diss., University of Tennessee, 1977).*

Chapter 1
Pocahontas: The Historical Record

8 *For Indian appearance and daily life, see Helen C. Rountree,* The Powhatan Indians of Virginia: Their Traditional Culture *(Norman, Okla., and London, 1989), pp. 32-78; Helen C. Rountree,* Pocahontas's People: The Powhatan Indians of Virginia through Four Centuries *(Norman, Okla., and London, 1990), pp. 3-14; Strachey,* Virginia Britannia, *p. 65 (quotations).*

9 *Strachey,* Virginia Britannia, *p. 66; Philip L. Barbour, ed.,* The Jamestown Voyages under the First Charter, 1606-1609, *Works issued by the Hakluyt Society, 2d ser., 136, 137 (2 vols.; Cambridge, 1969), p. 142; Rountree,* Powhatan Indians, *p. 76.*

10 *Strachey,* Virginia Britannia, *p. 57.*

11 *Ibid., p. 66.*

Chapter 2
Episodes from the Life of Pocahontas

12 *Barbour, ed.,* Complete Works of Smith, *1:63, 213.*

13 *Barbour, ed.,* Complete Works of Smith, *2:146-52, 259. The capture of Smith—without mention of the rescue—is related as well in Smith's* True Relation *(1608) and his* Proceedings *(1612); see Barbour, ed.,* Complete Works of Smith, *1:45-61, 212.*

14 *Barbour, ed.,* Complete Works of Smith, *2:146, 1:47.*

15 *Ibid., 2:150.*

16 *Ibid., 1:53, 2:150-51.*

[17] *Ibid., 2:147.*

[18] *Ibid., 2:150.*

[19] *John Davis,* The Farmer of New Jersey, or, A Picture of Domestic Life *(New York, 1800), pp. 10-11; John Davis,* Travels Of Four Years And A Half In The United States Of America During 1798, 1799, 1800, 1801, And 1802, *ed. A. J. Morrison (1803; New York, 1909), p. 321; John Davis,* Captain Smith and Pocahontas, An Indian Tale *(Philadelphia, 1805); John Davis,* The First Settlers of Virginia: An Historical Novel *(New York, 1805). See also Tilton,* Pocahontas, *chap. 2.*

[20] *Davis,* Travels Of Four Years And A Half in The United States, *p. 321.*

[21] *John Burk,* The History of Virginia from Its First Settlement to the Present Day *(4 vols.; Petersburg, 1804), 1:187.*

[22] *James Nelson Barker,* The Indian Princess *(Philadelphia, 1808).*

[23] *Vivien Green Fryd,* Art & Empire: The Politics of Ethnicity in the United States Capitol, 1815-1860 *(New Haven and London, 1992), p. 23.*

[24] *The popular prints of the rescue are discussed by Abrams in "The Pocahontas Paradox," p. 6.*

[25] *William Gilmore Simms,* Views and Reviews in American Literature, History and Fiction, *ed. C. Hugh Holman (1845; Cambridge, 1962), pp. 112-27.*

[26] *Account books of John Gadsby Chapman, courtesy of Robert Mayo, their owner. A damaged copy of the print is owned by the New-York Historical Society. Chapman's image is crudely reproduced in Robert Sears,* The Pictorial History of the American Revolution *(New York, 1856).*

[27] *Simms,* Views and Reviews, *pp. 115, 119-20.*

[28] *Ibid., pp. 119-20.*

[29] *Chappel exhibited* Pocahontas Saving John Smith *at the Brooklyn Art Association in 1861 (information courtesy of Clark S. Marlor).*

[30] *The painting measures 89 by 74 1/2 inches and is owned by the Brigham Young University Museum of Art.*

[31] *Henry Adams,* The Education of Henry Adams, *(Boston, 1918), p. 222. Adams confided his intentions to Palfrey in a letter of 20 March 1862. See J. C. Levenson et al., eds.,* The Letters of Henry Adams *(2 vols.; Cambridge, Mass., 1982), 1:287. The anti-Smith article appeared in* North American Review *104 (1867): 1-30.*

[32] *See Rountree,* Pocahontas's People, *pp. 38-39; Rountree,* Powhatan Indians, *pp. 116-17.*

[33] *See Philip L. Barbour,* Pocahontas and Her World *(Boston, 1970), pp. 24-25.*

[34] *These arguments are derived from J.A. Leo Lemay,* Did Pocahontas Save Captain John Smith? *(Athens, Ga., and London, 1992).*

[35] *Barbour, ed.,* Complete Works of Smith, *1:274, 2:192-99, 259.*

[36] *See the account books of John Gadsby Chapman. If the* small Rescue *and* The Capture *survive, their present location is not known.* The Coronation of Powhatan *is owned by the Greenville County Museum of Art, Greenville, S.C.*

[37] *Account books of John Gadsby Chapman (the patron was H. Gilliat of New York City); Barbour, ed.,* Complete Works of Smith, *2:195, 198-99.*

[38] *Barbour, ed.,* Complete Works of Smith, *2:192.*

[39] *Ibid., 2:193, 195.*

[40] *Ibid., 2:197-99.*

[41] *Ibid., 2:203-4.*

[42] *Ibid., 1:xlix, 2:232.*

[43] *Samuel Purchas, comp.,* Hakluytus Posthumus, or Purchas His Pilgrimes . . . *(20 vols.; New York, 1906), 19:90-94; Ralph Hamor,* A True Discourse of the Present Estate of Virginia *(1615; Richmond, 1957), pp. 4-11; Barbour, ed.,* Complete Works of Smith, *2:243-45; N. E. McClure, ed.,* The Letters of John Chamberlain *(2 vols.; Philadelphia, 1939), 1:470.*

[44] *McClure, ed.,* Letters of Chamberlain, *1:470.*

[45] *Purchas, comp.,* Purchas His Pilgrimes, *19:92-93; Ralph Hamor,* A True Discourse of the Present State of Virginia . . . , *ed. A. L. Rowse (1615; Richmond, 1957), p. 5.*

[46] *Hamor,* True Discourse, *pp. 5-6.*

[47] *Purchas, comp.,* Purchas His Pilgrimes, *19:93-94.*

[48] *Barbara J. Mitnick,* Jean Leon Gerome Ferris, 1863-1930: American Painter Historian *(Laurel, Miss., 1985), entry 8.*

[49] *Purchas, comp.,* Purchas His Pilgrimes, *19:94; Hamor,* True Discourse, *p. 7.*

[50] *Hamor,* True Discourse, *p. 9; Barbour, ed.,* Complete Works of Smith, *2:245.*

[51] *Hamor,* True Discourse, *p. 10.*

[52] *Ibid., pp. 48-69; (Dale's and Whitaker's letters are addressed to acquaintances in London ["To the R. and my most esteemed friend Mr. D. M. at his house at F. Ch. in London" and "To my verie deere and loving*

cosen M. G. Minister of the B. F. in London"], and Rolfe's letter is addressed to Dale); Barbour, ed., Complete Works of Smith, *2:251, 258.*

53 *Fryd,* Art & Empire, *pp. 45-46.*

54 *Hamor,* True Discourse, *pp. 55-56.*

55 *Barbour, ed.,* Complete Works of Smith, *2:258.*

56 *See Harry Culverwell Porter, "Alexander Whitaker: Cambridge Apostle to Virginia,"* William and Mary Quarterly, *3d ser., 14 (1957): 317-43.*

57 *Hamor,* True Discourse, *pp. 59-60.*

58 *For the trip to England, see Georgia Stamm Chamberlain,* Studies on John Gadsby Chapman *(Annandale, Va., 1963), pp. 19-20; for the search in Virginia, see John Gadsby Chapman's letters 28 Nov. 1837, 27 Jan., 13 Mar. 1838, William Bolling Papers, Virginia Historical Society.*

59 *Chamberlain,* Chapman, *p. 18.*

60 The Picture of the Baptism of Pocahontas. Painted by Order of Congress, For the Rotundo of the Capitol, by J. G. Chapman, of Washington *(Washington, D.C., 1840), p. 8, and facing p. 8 (key to the painting). See also Chapman's journal with notes about Jamestown history, owned by Jamestown Settlement.*

61 Picture of the Baptism, *pp. 3-5.*

62 *Ibid., p. 6.*

63 *For further discussion of the baptism of Pocahontas, see Tilton,* Pocahontas, *chap. 4.*

64 *Barbour, ed.,* Complete Works of Smith, *2:258.*

65 *Hamor,* True Discourse, *pp. 64, 66.*

66 *Ibid., p. 55.*

67 *For Hawthorne's comments, see Thomas Woodson, ed.,* The French and Italian Notebooks *(Columbus, Ohio, 1980), pp. 153-54.*

68 *For another interpretation, that of Pocahontas's "willingness to forego temporal power for the sacrificial spiritual power of the woman's sphere," see Joy S. Kasson, "Power and Powerlessness: Death, Sexuality and the Demonic in Nineteenth-Century American Sculpture,"* Women's Studies *15 (1988): 355.*

69 *Hamor,* True Discourse, *pp. 10-11, 48-69; Barbour, ed.,* Complete Works of Smith, *2:245-46; Strachey,* Virginia Britannia, *p. 54.*

70 *Hamor,* True Discourse, *pp. 63-67.*

71 *Benson J. Lossing,* The Marriage of Pocahontas *(New York, 1855). The Virginia Historical Society's copy of this pamphlet has stamped on its cover "Nusbaum's," the name of a print seller in Norfolk, Virginia— evidence that the print was marketed in Virginia.*

72 *Ibid., p. 5.*

73 *Hamor,* True Discourse, *p. 55.*

74 *Hamor,* True Discourse, *p. 11; Barbour, ed.,* Complete Works of Smith, *2:246.*

75 *For a concise history of the early years of the Jamestown settlement, see Rountree,* Pocahontas's People, *pp. 29-65.*

76 *Lossing,* Marriage of Pocahontas, *pp. 4-5.*

77 *McClure, ed.,* Letters of Chamberlain, *1:470, 2:12, 50, 57, 66; Purchas, comp.,* Purchas His Pilgrimes, *19:90-94; Barbour, ed.,* Complete Works of Smith, *2:260-62.*

78 *Barbour, ed.,* Complete Works of Smith, *2:261.*

79 *McClure, ed.,* Letters of Chamberlain, *2:50.*

80 *Robert Beverley,* The History and Present State of Virginia, *ed. Louis B. Wright (1705; Chapel Hill, 1947), p. 44.*

81 *Purchas, comp.,* Purchas His Pilgrimes, *19:118.*

82 *The college was to have been located at Henrico, site of the Rolfe family home. See David R. Ransome, "Pocahontas and the Mission to the Indians," Virginia* Magazine of History and Biography *99 (1991): 81-94.*

83 *McClure, ed.,* Letters of Chamberlain, *2:57. The earrings are owned by the Association for the Preservation of Virginia Antiquities.*

84 *Barbour, ed.,* Complete Works of Smith, *2:260-61. See Karen Robertson, "Pocahontas at the Masque," paper delivered at the meeting of the Shakespeare Association of America, Philadelphia, April 12, 1990.*

85 *Barbour, ed.,* Complete Works of Smith, *2:262.*

Chapter 3
The Legend of Pocahontas

86 *McClure, ed.,* Letters of Chamberlain, *1:57; Barbour, ed.,* Complete Works of Smith, *2:261.*

87 *The letter is printed in the 17-24 June 1734 edition; it is reprinted in Lawrence W. Towner, "Ars Poetica et Sculptura: Pocahontas on the Boston Common,"* Journal of Southern History *28 (1962): 484-85.*

88 *Extensive research on the Turkey Island portrait and Robert Matthew Sully's interest in the Pocahontas theme has been conducted by Cleo Mullins, who began her study of this subject when she conserved*

the Virginia Historical Society's painting of *Pocahontas* by the younger Sully and whose findings are borrowed here.

89 *John Gadsby Chapman to William Bolling, 27 Jan. 1838, William Bolling Papers.*

90 *William Bolling, statement, May 1838, William Bolling Papers; Linnaeus Bolling to William Bolling, 14 Sept. 1830, ibid.; Richmond* Enquirer, *3, 28 Sept. 1830.*

91 *John Gadsby Chapman to William Bolling, 27 Jan. 1838, William Bolling Papers.*

92 *Richmond* Enquirer, *10, 17 Sept. 1830.*

93 *R. M. Sully to Lyman C. Draper, 20 Apr. 1854, n.d. Apr. 1854, Draper and Wisconsin State Historical Society Papers. Sully sold paintings to the Historical Society of Wisconsin and planned to relocate in Madison, only to die on the journey there.*

94 *R. M. Sully to Lyman C. Draper, 13 May 1854, State Historical Society of Wisconsin; for R. M. Sully's account of the authenticity of the engraving from which his portrait of Pocahontas was painted, see State Historical Society of Wisconsin (Misc. Doc. No. 18, SC 1709, Mar. 1855).*

95 *R. M. Sully to Lyman C. Draper, 13 May 1854, State Historical Society of Wisconsin.*

96 *R. M. Sully to Lyman C. Draper, n.d. Oct. 1854, State Historical Society of Wisconsin.*

97 *J. E. C. [John Esten Cooke], "Wanderings on the Banks of the York,"* Southern Literary Messenger *26 (June 1858): 457-65.*

98 *See the discussion of Pocahontas in sectionalist propaganda in Tilton,* Pocahontas, *pp. 4-5, and chap. 5.*

99 *William Hillhouse,* Pocahontas; A Proclamation: With Plates *(New Haven, 1820), p. 12; Pocahontas [Emily Clemens Pearson],* Cousin Franck's Household, or, Scenes in the Old Dominion *(4th ed.; Boston, 1853).*

100 *John Esten Cooke, "A Dream of the Cavaliers,"* Harper's New Monthly Magazine *27 (Jan. 1861): 252-54.*

101 *J. F. Lay, "Reminiscences of the Powhatan Troop of Cavalry in 1861,"* Southern Historical Society Papers *8 (1880): 418-26. The Powhatan Guards ceased to carry the ceremonial flag after the unit became a part of the 4th Virginia Cavalry later in 1861.*

102 *See the* Dictionary of American Naval Fighting Ships *(8 vols.; Washington, D.C., 1959-81), 5:s.v.; William Armstrong Fairburn,* Merchant Sail *(6 vols.; Center Lovell, Maine, 1944-55), 2:1026-27.*

103 *Linda Bantel,* William Rush, American Sculptor *(Philadelphia, 1992), pp. 180-81.*

104 *John Esten Cooke,* My Lady Pokahontas . . . *(Boston and New York, 1885).*

105 *Wyndham Robertson,* Pocahontas alias Matoaka and Her Descendants *(Richmond, 1887). William Wirt Henry published a number of pieces in defense of John Smith and Pocahontas. See, for example, William Wirt Henry, "The Rescue of Captain John Smith by Pocahontas,"* Potters American Monthly *4-5 (1875): 523-28, 591-97; "The Settlement at Jamestown, With Particular Reference to the Late Attacks upon Captain Smith, Pocahontas, and John Rolfe,"* Proceedings of the Virginia Historical Society *(Richmond, 1882), pp. 10-62; "A Defence of Captain John Smith,"* Magazine of American History *25 (1891): 300-313; "Did Percy Denounce Smith's History of Virginia?"* Virginia Magazine of History and Biography *1 (1893-94): 473-76.*

106 *Adolphe Bandelier to Thomas Janvier, 2 Sept. 1888, in* The Unpublished Letters of Adolphe F. Bandelier *(El Paso, 1942), p. 3.*

107 *Lyon G. Tyler,* Pocahontas, Peace and Truth *(Richmond, 1915), pp. 7, 14.*

108 *Mrs. John B. Lightfoot, "Statue of Pocahontas Unveiled after 16 Years of Splendid Effort,"* Sons of the Revolution in State of Virginia Quarterly Magazine *1 (July 1922): 23.*

109 *"Monument to Pocahontas at Jamestown, Va.,"* U.S. Senate Report No. 1073, 62d Congress, 3d Session. *Federal funding was sought to provide the remaining $5,000 of the commission, but Senate Bill 2118 ("A bill to aid in the erection of a monument to Pocahontas at Jamestown, Va.") did not pass.*

110 *A Kentuckian [James Chamberlayne Pickett],* The Memory of Pocahontas Vindicated Against the Erroneous Judgment of the Hon. Waddy Thompson . . . *(Washington, D.C., 1847), p. 5.*

111 *Richard B. Sherman, "'The Last Stand': The Fight for Racial Integrity in Virginia in the 1920s,"* Journal of Southern History *54 (1988): 74, 77.*

112 *James M. Lindgren,* Preserving the Old Dominion: Historic Preservation and Virginia Traditionalism *(Charlottesville and London, 1993), pp. 29, 132-33.*

113 *Ibid., pp. 132-33.*

114 *Ibid., p. 132.*

115 *Edith Sale,* Old Time Belles and Cavaliers *(Philadelphia and London, 1912), p. 12.*

116 *Mimi C. Miley,* Howard Chandler Christy, Artist/Illustrator of Style *(Allentown, Pa., 1977), n.p.*

[117] *Howard Chandler Christy, ed.,* Liberty Belles: Eight Epochs in the Making of the American Girl *(Indianapolis, 1912). Selections of poetry by prominent poets accompany the pictures by Christy. Not one of the other "Liberty Belles" ("The Puritan Girl," "The Colonial Girl," "The Revolutionary Girl," "The Pioneer Girl," "The Dixie Girl," "The Western Girl," and "The American Girl") is identified as a specific person. Pocahontas, because of her well-established fame, stands in a class by herself.*

[118] *Mitnick,* Ferris, *entry 9.*

[119] *Miley,* Christy, *plate 34. The canvas is large, 36 by 40 inches.*

[120] *Conversation and correspondence with Alicia Weber of the Fine Arts Program of the General Services Administration. See also Lincoln Kirstein,* Paul Cadmus *(New York, 1984), pp. 36-37.*

Epilogue

[121] *Vachel Lindsay, "Our Mother Pocahontas," in* The Chinese Nightingale and Other Poems *(New York, 1917), p. 40. The poet renounces the "Saxon blood" and "Teuton pride" of the white race.*